Praise for Winning

"Those of us that have spent our lives training and mentoring salespeople know that the way a person THINKS will almost completely seal their fate. The authors of Winning Sales Attitudes take you down a path that exposes and explains the key mindsets you'll need to thrive in a commission sales venture. Great job, Joe and team!"

—**WILLIAM "TRIPP" AMOS,** Chairman – Piedmont Payment Services

"Any of us that have sold ourselves and our products know that the longest distance we'll have to travel is that SIX inches between our ears. The authors that Joe invited to be part of this book are hard-core sales pros, and they've shared incredible mindsets that all salespeople need to emulate and practice."

—**LEEZA CARLONE STEINDORF,** Coach, trainer, speaker, mediator–Forbes Coaches Council member, Tony Robbins Results Coach, award-winning author

"This book is written by ROCKSTAR salespeople FOR those who wish to become masters at their craft. There's pure gold for the sales mind between the covers. Grab this book!"

—**ERIC SILVERMAN,** Founder – Voluntary Disruption

"Winning Sales Attitudes offers you a blueprint of how to think and respond to almost every scenario in sales. Anybody who's sold anything knows that the right ATTITUDE comes first...then success follows. This book is a treasure of wisdom by a handful of great sales masters!"

—**BILL CATES,** CSP, CPAE, Hall of Fame Speaker and author of Beyond Referrals and Radical Relevance

"Leadership books are generally as relevant as the people who write them and the track record they have in leading people. This book not only comes with a strong track record of authors and leaders, but it also provides practical strategies to help any leader to do the same, regardless of their experience level."

—**Kelsey Evert,** Legacy sales and thought leader

"One of my favorite authors has done it again! In his latest book, Winning Sales Attitudes: The key mindsets all great salespeople adopt and practice on their path to wealth, Joe Buzzello has assembled a team of some of the brightest sales leaders across the U.S. Together they guide you through a collection of some of the most valuable lessons you must master in building a hugely successful sales career. This book is filled with great stories of real-life examples and is a wonderfully enjoyable reading experience. But most importantly, when you read, internalize and apply the lessons you'll find inside–you too will develop those Winning Sales Attitudes and your sales career will skyrocket!"

—**Jeff C. West,** Author of the award winning sales fable, *The Unexpected Tour Guide;* former Aflac State Sales Coordinator, founder of *Fusion Points: Engage The Science of Persistence*

"In his fourth release, Joe takes his years of experience and he combines that with his vast network of entrepreneurs and sales professionals. What he created is an impactful and entertaining book that is a MUST read. The Cap Equation methodology and Winning Sales Attitudes are incredible tools and resources for a salesperson that wants to win big-time."

—**Gary Ware,** President – Ware Group General Agencies

"I've been around many great salespeople and sales leaders during my decades of service, but Joe is one of the very best. With the vehicle of this book, he's been able to harness the experience and wisdom of so many others that also fall into that 'great' category. An AMAZING sales book! Get it...and practice ALL of what you read, and your income will grow!"

—**Andy Glaub,** Senior Vice President, Director of U.S. Sales – Aflac

"I have been selling for over two decades, and I've never read a book that instructs on the sales mindset as well as this one does. Joe has attracted a phenomenal team of authors and this is a GEM. READ it...and more importantly, PRACTICE these key attitudes."

—**MICHAEL RHODD,** Managing Partner – PCS Advisers, Inc.

"Winning Sales Attitudes nails it. After a certain point of your skillset development, it's ALL about your attitude—how you think your way through your day, week and month. This is the most prolific book I've ever read on this topic! Great job, Joe and contributors."

—**GEORGE KIEF, JR.,** Managing Partner – Western Component Sales

"I've been around Joe and his sales process practices for a few years now. Take my word for it...the methods he and his CAP Equation Certified Instructors teach are golden. If you consider yourself a true sales professional, then this book has to be on your must read list."

—**DR. PAUL FLATLEY,** Founder – Direct2MD

"Joe has done it again. But this time he brought some other big talent along with him. Winning Sales Attitudes is a compilation of some of the finest content ever written on the subject of how your attitude determines your ultimate results. This book is a MASTER CLASS in sales mindsets. Kudos to all of these great contributors!"

—**LES HEINSEN,** Founder – Element 79 Vineyards

"The best and the brightest salespeople simply outthink the competition. You want to achieve better results and earn higher commissions? Read this book."

—**MARC EMMER,** President – Optimize, Inc.

"We're all selling something...a product, service or a vision for something better. Winning Sales Attitudes is a MUST read for anyone focused on improving their sales process. The Sales Maestro himself, Joe Buzzello, guides us through dozens of CRITICAL mindsets presented by the co-authors. These concepts will change the way you think about the game of sales. Make sure ALL of your salespeople have a copy of this book!"

—**BRYAN MCLAREN,** Chief Executive Officer – Zoned Properties, Inc.

"We can hire experienced salespeople with ample skillsets, but the right headspace is much harder to identify and teach. In his fourth book, Winning Sales Attitudes, Joe and his selected co-authors do an amazing job instructing on all of the key attitudes that we know a sales pro needs to have immense success at their role. This book is a sales mindset bible!"

—**MATT WALSH,** Founder – Blue Signal Search

"This is the perfect sales-related book for these times! If you want to change your position it begins with what you're thinking."

—**MARK HUNTER,** "The Sales Hunter"

"All of us that live and breathe the science of selling know that the mindset we carry into the game is critical. The contributors of Winning Sales Attitudes blueprint the way top producers consistently think and behave. A great read—and easy stuff to apply."

—**ANTHONY IANNARINO,** Bestselling author, salesman, speaker and sales leader

"Joe has an ability to connect with his audience in a very straight-forward and easy going way that makes, Winning Sales Attitudes a must read and an archetype for the science of sales. His co-authors are also big shining stars!"

—**CAPTAIN DOUG FOX,** CEO & Founder – Foxy's Custom Cruises

"Great attitudes are critical to personal growth and the growth of an organization, especially in the area of business development. I've not seen a collection of master salespeople come together like this before to draft an entire book of key sales-related MINDSETS. What they teach you in this book can easily be applied to your business today...and your results will improve!"

—**CASEY STRUNK,** President – The Strunk Insurance Group

"As small business owners, we know our products well and we have solid skillsets when it comes to selling them. In this book, Winning Sales Attitudes, you'll learn the OTHER side of the selling equation—how to manage your attitudes, emotions and mindsets. Joe Buzzello and his fellow authors have documented a treasure of proven methods you can begin to apply right now."

—**SHAINA WEISINGER,** Founder & CEO – RepurposeHouse.com

"Rarely do we find such a tremendous collaboration of talent and mastery in one place. Joe has assembled true sales winners who are also winners at the game of life. Treat yourself to this one!"

—**ANDY GRETHEL,** Maestro Health

"Joe has curated the wisdom of many sales pros, and they've masterfully described the behaviors that put you in a position to WIN in the game of sales. This book is full of so many golden nuggets; you'll read it again and again to ensure you mine them all. Great stuff!"

—**ADAM MICHAELS,** Visionary leader,
entrepreneur, Founder – Enrollify

"As a person who networks and communicates with humans constantly—inviting them to become part of our 'tribe'—I'm completely aware of my headspace. Winning Sales Attitudes is a book 100% DEDICATED to our sales-related mindsets. What a wonderful gift to newer salespeople... and also some of us 'veterans' that need to be reminded of how to guard our good attitudes."

—**GELIE,** Entrepreneur, community leader, TEDx Presenter,
mentor, momma and Founder – NetworkingPhoenix.com

I have had had the pleasure of meeting and working with many of the co-authors and contributors featured in this great book. They are all-world sales PROs. For them to all come together with Joe to record their thoughts about the key ATTITUDES necessary to win in sales is pretty special. Do yourself a favor and grab this book!"

—**TOM HEALY,** author, speaker, Co-Founder + CEO
of LaunchPoint, Co-Founder of Growth10

WINNING
SALES
Attitudes

WINNING
SALES
Attitudes

The key mindsets all great
salespeople adopt and practice
on their path to wealth

JOE BUZZELLO

CHUCK FARMER   SCOTT STORJOHANN   EMILY EVANS
BRANDEE JUSTUS   DAWN TYACK   CHRISTIE MARZARI
DENNIS HARTIN   LEON DAVIDSON   RENEE CORSO
KATIE ANDERSON   TRACI BATTEN

Creative, LLC

ISBN: 978-0-9969503-2-9

This book is dedicated to:

James R. "Jimmy" Hill

God rest his soul!

I've never met anyone in sales (and life) that had a better attitude and was more positive than Jimmy. He was a dear friend to so many of us. He was a key mentor for me—saving my career...twice! (A story for another time)

Table of Contents

Section 3
Risk, Change, Urgency + Objectives

Section 4
Coachability, The Work + Accountability

Section 5
Emotional Controls, Humility + Self Talk

Section 6
Focus + Execution

Section 7
Time

Introduction

The problem with a "ten-cent head"

"The longest distance a new salesperson will ever have to travel is the six inches between their own two ears."

—Joe Buzzello

This book is the long awaited sequel to **The CAP Equation**. Just over five years have elapsed since the writing of that book (my first book) and many good things have happened in my life and in my business. I've written and published two more books, **Drawing Circles**, a novel based on actual events, and **A Life in Sales**, Volume 1. In addition to writing these books, it has been my good fortune to have spoken to and conducted training at over one hundred and twenty organizations across the country. I have also launched two new successful business ventures, an online business that serves salespeople, entrepreneurs and leaders and a small business CEO/Founder peer advisory community based in Scottsdale. I've also added a few more pounds around the midsection and a few more gray hairs!

I've been busy.

And because I've never met a great idea I wouldn't try (not a great hab-it), in the spring of 2019 I launched a new program that I'd been contem-plating for some time. The idea came to me externally. A number of CAP Equation fans planted a thought in my head. It sounded something like this; "Hey, Joe. Why don't you create a formal certification around The CAP Equation sales methodology?" When umpteenth people all urged me to do the same thing, I decided that it might be a good idea.

I'm slow!

So the CAP Equation Certified Instructor (**CECI**) professional des-ignation was born! I drafted the curriculum and then went about the task of interviewing what would become our founding CECI group. As we began our virtual meetings and held our first live gathering in Arizona, I let the group know that I was interested in collaborating on a book for each of the **integers** that make CAP. Eleven people in our talented group stepped forward and contributed their expertise to this book, Winning Sales Attitudes.

If you are following along, this sequel represents the "A" in The **CAP** Equation...ATTITUDES. This book focuses on the headspace of a newer salesperson. But let me back up a moment...just in case you have NOT read The CAP Equation.

Back to the Future

Allow me to put you in the DeLorean and take you back to May of 1980. I was, nineteen years old and had just been promoted to field trainer for Pennsylvania Life. We sold $39 a year accident policies door to door—B2B. They told me I had to spend a day in the field with their #1 sales manager, John Jamelkowski, *the Polish Assassin...the Machine*.

John had flown F-4 fighters in Vietnam. He went about his day much like I imagine he went about a mission—total precision—no wasted time, energy or emotion. He ran level and he ran hard. He worked my ass off. We walked into forty doors before we stopped for lunch. When we did stop to eat, it was at an outdoor chilidog stand in Camarillo, CA. He ordered three dogs. I ordered one. He was finishing his last dog, and I was only halfway done with my first. I was supposed to ask him questions about his sales training and leadership philosophies. He was checking his watch—wanting to get back into the car—he had very little patience for small talk.

I was running out of time.

The reason they wanted me to spend a day in the field with John was that he was the most efficient sales trainer the company had. He got more salespeople into production than anybody else. He also got them deeper into production and retained more agents than anyone else.

He was truly a machine!

They wanted me to see him in action.

As he was wiping the chili from his chin, I asked if he would share some of his philosophies with me. He seemed perturbed, but at the same time, I could see him puff up a little bit. We all like to pontificate about what we do well, right?

So he went off.

But it was quick and I had to listen fast.

He said something like: (And I am closely quoting)

"It's like this buddy boy. There are only three reasons a salesperson might fail. First, they can fail if they don't say the right things. Secondly, they have to say those things in the right WAY—they need to hold their head up high. And if they DO know what to say, and HOW to say it, then they still need to see enough people, because if they don't see enough people it won't make any difference what they say or how they say it. They will still fail. They have to do all three of those things to ensure success."

"That's it, buddy. It's not complex."

And with that, he was done.

Mr. Jamelkowski didn't squander a lot of words.

He made his way back to the Cadillac El Dorado he drove. I wasn't far behind. I quizzed him again when we got back into the car—I asked him to iterate on his little hypothesis. He began to talk about the difference between two specific types of salespeople. He described the salesperson that knew what to say—had all of the sales skills wired—a slick tongued devil—but had faulty, poor mindsets and attitudes. Then he contrasted that with the new salesperson that possibly struggled a little bit with the pitch and the close. He indicated to me that he'd much rather work with a person who had a great **attitude**—reasoning that he could teach them the needed skillsets. He rationalized that if they had good skillsets, but didn't have a "good head," they were useless to him. He spoke of a new recruit that he'd been out in the field with a few times. He seemed to appreciate the guy's skills, but despised the guy's work habits. He portrayed the dude this way...

> **"...Look, I'm not sure what's with this guy, but he's got a million dollar mouth and a ten-cent head."**

I was starting to get it.

His little diatribe at the chilidog place was sinking in. What I heard John saying was that WHAT to say (**competencies** or skillsets) was a critical element. John was also pointing out that saying things in the **right way** (**attitudes** and mindsets) was an essential piece of the puzzle. Then he completed his trilogy of wisdom by suggesting that you have to see enough people. (A full **pipeline**) More importantly, I understood him to be telling me that if any of the three integers of his equation were missing, a salesperson might (or would) fail. Of course, the inverse result of this equation has to also be true. If a salesperson were firing on all three of those cylinders, they'd almost be assured of unlimited success.

> **"...The inverse result of this equation has to also be true. If a salesperson were firing on all three of those cylinders, they'd almost be assured of unlimited success."**

It took weeks, months, years and decades for me to perfect my thinking and practices. However, after that little chilidog epiphany anything and everything I did with regard to sales training and leadership revolved around those **three** sacred areas that John helped me identify:

- Competencies
- Attitudes
- Pipeline Practices

So, **The CAP Equation** sales methodology (A Foolproof Formula for Unlimited Success in Sales) was born, and refined and taught and shared and ripped off and duplicated.

It's all good...it's great to be excellent enough to be copied!

But this is the real stuff.

And for the first time in any medium, you're not only going to hear from me, you are also going to have the opportunity to learn from some of the best and brightest sales pros and trainers I know. Our co-authors are ardent CAP Equation followers (and instructors – **CECI'**) who have used many elements of our methodology to build their wealth. Most importantly, they have helped countless others launch and generate awesome careers in our great sales game.

THE PROBLEM WITH A "TEN-CENT HEAD"

With this first of three planned sequels to The CAP Equation, we're going to dive into the "A" in the CAP. I do have to tell you that *attitudes* jumped to the forefront as the **CECI'** group and I began to discuss which one of the three integers we'd write about first.

When I instructed our **CECI'** group to begin submitting their ideas for training topics and themes for all three categories, it was surprising. The work that was submitted for attitudes was almost **triple** the other two areas.

The "A" just seemed to win the day!

So I advised the group that the book on attitudes and mindsets would happen first. Then I went about the task of helping them shape their ideas so they flowed well on paper and made sense. We collaborated on most of the chapters. I only wrote a few of them myself. I do have to tell you that the collaboration was so much fun for me. (I had never done this before) We sent rough thoughts and chapter drafts back and forth—editing on the fly until the chapters felt right.

Tons of fun!

But let me address why I think we had so many attitude related submissions...I believe that all great sales trainers and coaches believe the same thing that John Jamelkowski believed. When a salesperson has a, "ten-cent head," you simply can't do all that much to help them. In fact they may even **undo** anything good you do for them. We all feel that competencies and pipeline practices can be easily taught and transferred to a salesperson, especially if they have a great attitude about things. But if you are dealing with a mental and emotional basket case, you're dead in the water as a trainer, coach or mentor. We all seem to want to jump into this area with both feet, because in our heart of hearts, we know that there is a certain set of attitudes and mindsets that, if mastered, make it nearly impossible for a salesperson to fail if they'll just show up and go to work.

> *"...There is a certain set of attitudes and mindsets that, if mastered, make it nearly impossible for a salesperson to fail if they'll just show up and go to work."*

So, there ya go.

The problem with a "ten-cent head" is you just can't progress in sales if you own one. You'll implode, self-destruct and crash and burn sooner or later—probably sooner.

With this book we endeavor to walk you through a number of key and essential mindsets and attitudes that all great salespeople **adopt** and **practice**, sooner than later.

And then they **survive**.

And eventually they **thrive**.

And some go on to become **mentors** to others.

Which we love to see!

So, enjoy what these great CAP Equation Certified Instructors and I have put together for you. Let's go **WIN together** by having you emulate all of the great attitudes that we outline in this book.

Joe Buzzello
Scottsdale, Arizona
April 2020

Section 1

Purpose, Passion + Vision

Developing key mindsets about **WHY** *you do what you do and* **WHERE** *you wish to take your business and career.*

CHAPTER 1

Your Path to "WHY"

Developing an attitude of PURPOSE

CHRISTIE MARZARI WITH JOE BUZZELLO

"When you know your WHY, your WHAT has more
impact because you're walking IN your purpose."

—MICHAEL JR.

Why in the world would you jump into commission-only sales?
Why would you work so damn hard **without** a salary?

Why would you subject yourself to the constant disappointment
of, "NO"?

Why would you put in **all that time and effort** on faith, with no guarantees whatsoever?

These are great questions and they deserve to be answered. More importantly, if you don't recognize why you're willing to get into a commission sales gig—one where there are no guarantees and a heap of rejection—you may not stick and stay long enough to get over the hump.

What we're going to focus on in this chapter is how you may go about the task of determining what the heck your purpose really is at this moment. We believe your WHY is a path and a process. We know that your purpose can (and will) *shift* based on the season of your life, and your maturity level.

Let's take a look at three important factors that are in play.

The Money

Let's get real for a minute.

We can dance around this one until we're dizzy, but the big money you can pull down in commission sales is always a factor. Ya gotta' pay the bills, right? So let's just accept the fact that (to some level) **we do this for the money**. When we were kids, very few of us said, "Hey, when I grow up I wanna' get into commission sales because constant rejection sounds like fun." LOL! Think about it, the job hardly makes sense on the surface. You work mostly in isolation, pounding the phone or the streets a good portion of your work hours. You must place yourself in harms way, cold calling—facing numerous non-responses, turndowns and blow-offs. You toil in seclusion, looking for that elusive, "YES." The sales game may also feel extremely awkward for most people—learning particular phrasing and questions that have to be delivered in a certain way, and with specific timing. Worse, you typically do all of this work with no base of income.

We are aware that there are outliers—people who are supremely gifted. These outliers have oodles of natural ability—the sort of people that can sell ice cubes to Eskimos. The rest of us have to **painfully develop skillsets** and mindsets—nurture them over long periods of time.

So, this thing we call "sales" is hard.

Ultimately, most people don't get involved in commission sales if they don't think they can pull down a ton of money. But here's a small problem with the "money" thing—**MONEY isn't a reason**. It's merely an outcome or a result. It's not a purpose at all.

> *"...MONEY isn't a reason. It's merely an outcome*
> *or a result. It's not a purpose at all."*

If we robotically think or say, "I'm doing this for the money," we should probably peel another layer off of the onion—ask ourselves an additional question...

> *"What would I DO with all that money?*
> *How would it change my life?"*

If we respond, with answers such as, "I'd buy my first home," or, "I'd send my children to the best private schools," then we're getting to **the real WHY**. That's why we are doing this—because we want to accomplish that other thing.

The money is simply a **tool** or vehicle for us.

What we'll **DO** with all that money is the purpose.

So we begin with the MONEY thing...or better, **what the money will do for us**, then we evolve from there. We begin to realize that the business of sales is an amazing game. We become energized when we start to win and we receive recognition and awards. We get to tell our parents that, "Hey, this IS a real job, mom!" LOL! Those of us that have figured out how to handle the setbacks, pushbacks and all of the "NOs", can begin to advance our thinking. When we mature enough to learn how to control our emotions, and develop solid attitudes, we can then move from just making some money and paying the bills to finding something more in this game.

> *"When we mature enough to learn how to control*
> *our emotions, and develop solid attitudes, we can*
> *then move from just making some money and paying*
> *the bills to finding something more in this game."*

THE INTERNAL PURPOSES

As we move down the path to WHY a bit further, sales becomes more than just a great job that pays well.

The reality of it is that great salespeople thrive because of highly formed, positive attitudes. Another eternal truth is that our attitudes are driven by what we **tell** ourselves. Since over 80% of what we "hear" can be considered "self talk", then focusing on our passionate (internal) work is critical to monitoring and improving our inner monologue.

> *"...great salespeople thrive because of highly formed, positive attitudes."*

What do we tell ourselves about ourselves?

HOW can we make sales more than just a job so that we can run this marathon? Let's face it; there's no **high** like a salesperson's rush after they close a big deal and pocket a fat commission. Conversely, there's no *low* like a salesperson's disappointment when something they were counting on falls apart...and there's no paycheck.

This type of emotional roller coaster can burn you out quickly.

Even some of the best salespeople in our business can suffer from these dramatic mood swings unless they identify what they're **building** and what they wish to **become** in the process. We can dance around the various reasons we do this. Flexibility and freedom come to mind. Buying a new car or a bigger house also hits our radar. By all means—please pursue those material dreams. Keep those things in front of you every day. Write those things down; post them for all to see. Share those dreams with those you love. It would be awesome if they were BIG dreams and goals. The big things that are important to you will keep you fully engaged, even during the tough times. In fact, the bigger your dreams are, the better it is, because you'll silently acknowledge that these BIG things are well worth trading some temporary pain for.

> *"The big things that are important to you will keep you fully engaged, even during the tough times."*

But there's **one additional place** we want you to go...

We want you to begin to become very conscious of what you want to **BUILD**. What does that edifice look like? When people point to your career and business, what will the legacy of it say to the world?

Then...ask, "What do I wish to **BECOME** in the process?"

This **internal thing** is really about the personal and professional **growth** that will happen **INSIDE of you** as you are pursuing that new car, or bigger house or countless other material objects. This is the positive **change** and maturity that occurs internally as you build your business empire. This is quite a significant side benefit of making some money and buying a few toys.

Don't you agree?

THE EXTERNAL PURPOSES

This "external" part of your path to WHY is about your eyes going from inward to outward.

A friend of ours once said:

> *"I know a lot of salespeople that make money at the expense of others; but it is a true blessing to find an opportunity where you're able to make money WHILE helping others."*

This describes a rare, but rewarding fusion of purposes.

When you find a purpose that involves others, you grow beyond you—outside of yourself. What you **sell** and what you **do** can help and benefit an individual, a family, a company or a community. You have eventually reached a great place—a place where most of your needs are taken care of. Then your eyes slowly turn to others. You **add value** to others—to their businesses and lives and before you know it, you're creating a legacy.

> *"When you find a purpose that involves others, you grow beyond you—outside of yourself."*

In this chapter, we've challenged you to think about what your path to WHY may be, and how it can (and will) **evolve**. You have this wonderful opportunity sitting right in front of you. You can create a high-level career in sales, one where you can become a master of your craft, help yourself and help many other people in the process.

In order to run the long race you must navigate your path to WHY, and it has to be **more** than just turning a buck. Your WHY has to have more influence on you than just that. When you develop an attitude of PUR-POSE beyond money and material things, you will **live in** and **walk in** your purpose each day, and you'll have developed an incredible impact that will extend <u>beyond you</u> and take you farther than you've ever dreamed.

"In order to run the long race you must navigate your path to WHY, and it has to be more than just turning a buck."

Chapter 2

Employing Your WHY

A lighthouse in foul weather

Chuck Farmer with Joe Buzzello

*"You must start your career with specific and personal WHYs! Then you'll **FOCUS** on them when tough times come around...and tough times will come around."*

—Chuck Farmer

Your **WHY** is the reason you follow a certain course of action. It may be a new hobby, a financial plan, an exercise regimen, or a specific career pursuit. In this chapter we're going to take a look at what those reasons sound like and more importantly, how you can *employ* them as **directional tools** to keep your sales career on track.

Do you know what a lighthouse is?

In case you don't, a lighthouse is a towering structure with a rather strong light (and lens) that can be seen at quite a distance from sea. A lighthouse marks the safe entrance to a harbor. In darkness or foul weather, a skipper uses the light as a navigational aid to find the best path. If he follows the strong beam of light, his craft will reach its destination safely. If he misses the entrance to the harbor, crew and passengers may perish on the rocks. Other more current forms of maritime navigation (like GPS), have minimized the need for these iconic structures, but in many coastal areas, lighthouses are still in use and are still important to sailors at sea.

So we believe that your strong WHYs—your **reasons** for getting involved in commission sales—are exactly like those beacons of light emanating from a lighthouse. If they're strong and focused upon, you will reach your destination of income and career benchmarks successfully. Conversely, if your reasons for building a career in commission sales aren't clear, or not revisited often, you can easily lose your way as things get rough, and then you'll wind up crashing into the rocks—and drowning.

> *"...If your reasons for building a career in commission sales aren't clear...you can easily lose your way..."*

When Chuck Farmer interviews people for sales positions, he focuses on their "why". He asks several key questions about their motivations. He works hard to dig out answers from each prospective career candidate. In any given interview he may ask...

- *Why do you want to do this **type** of work?*
- *What would you like to **accomplish** in your career?*
- *Which aspects of commission sales appeal to you most?*
- *What personal **objectives** have you established for yourself?*
- *If you were to become ultra-successful, how would it **change your life**?*

Chuck tells his candidates about why his most successful salespeople originally joined his team. He tells **his story**—why he left a salaried position to begin a career in commission sales. Finally, he expresses to them why he has lasted so long in the game of commission sales. From the inception of his relationship with a new salesperson, Chuck is focused on helping that person develop his or her own personal WHY.

When he offers them a position, the first thing he does is spend a few minutes helping them solidify their personal reasons, both in their **minds** and in their **hearts**. Joe has said for many years that, "If your WHY is strong enough, the HOW takes care of itself."

> ### *"...If your WHY is strong enough, the HOW takes care of itself."*

Chuck doesn't stop there—he takes it deeper. In his new salesperson training classes he challenges them to *share* their **WHY** with the entire class. Hearing other new salespeople verbalize their reasons for entering the world of commission sales only solidifies their own WHY—again, in their hearts and minds.

Chuck and Joe have been at the game of coaching and mentoring salespeople for a combined sixty years. They know the power of the WHY and how important it is to help new salespeople identify and leverage it. They know that, in each and every career, there are **rough patches**. These tough times require a tough, gritty demeanor, but they can also be greatly mitigated if we keep our eye on the beam of light coming from the old lighthouse on shore.

Let's look at a few examples of WHY we (crazy) salespeople do what we do with a smile on our face:

CONTROL OF OUR OWN CALENDAR
(FREEDOM + FLEXIBILITY)

Most people (when they get real) will tell you that they value freedom and flexibility over a salary. People want the freedom to spend quality time with family and good friends. They want to enjoy leisure travel, engage in their favorite hobbies, volunteer for things that touch them, and sometimes they simply want to take a "me" day and relax.

Some people that have had to work nights, weekends and holidays for years feel like they've missed out while everyone else was enjoying a holiday or vacation. They had to meticulously plan their meager vacation days. Worse, they submitted a request and hoped it was approved.

What a great benefit **freedom** is. It's a powerful magnet, however there is one caveat that we warn people about. It's called the **Sword of Freedom**. We advise that the Sword of Freedom **cuts both ways**. We have the freedom to work as much as we'd like, or as little as we'd like. The **disciplines** that we apply to the flexibility of our schedule will determine our ultimate fate.

> ### "We have the freedom to work as much as we'd like, or as little as we'd like"

Even workaholics want to have control of their schedule. They may choose to work more days and hours than most, but they want to know that it's their choice—that a boss or higher authority didn't mandate it.

Helping People (Making a Difference)

It's amazing and uplifting to us how many of the people we've interviewed and hired have mentioned "helping people" as a passion of theirs. Even though the evening news features the worst stories about people, we've found that most people that aspire to have a sales career are friendly, nurturing people that truly care about others. Many tell us that "making a difference" in the lives of others fills a need for them. Even though the word, "salesman", may have negative connotations, we know that compassionate sales professionals can truly impact others' lives in a very positive manner.

Brian Gibson is a great salesperson that Chuck had the pleasure to mentor. Brian tells the story of handling his very first insurance claimant. A lady called his office asking for help with a cancer treatment claim. She mentioned that she didn't have the gas money to drive to his office, so Brian drove to her. She lived in an older trailer home that was in need of some repair. She explained to Brian that her husband was unable to work, and they had very little money. She asked Brian how much he thought they would receive. She told him that a thousand dollars would help them immensely. Brian promised that he would personally submit the claim and do everything he could to get her all of the money she had coming to her...and he'd do it as quickly as possible.

A few days later the claimant called Brian back. She was crying when Brian answered. He asked her what was wrong. She said, "Nothing was wrong." She explained that she had just received a check in the mail for over $17,000. She told Brian that they paid all their bills, bought groceries, and put gas in the car. She tearfully shared how she'd been able to enjoy a good night's sleep for the first time in years! Now that's an example of the kind of impact that a caring salesperson can have on others.

LONG-TERM WEALTH *(FINANCIAL SECURITY)*

A successful sales career will provide the earning potential and wealth that many only dream of. Think of all of the forms of compensation and perks that are available—commissions, production bonuses, residual income, stock or profit sharing, awards, paid trips to exotic locations, etc. While making "a lot of money" is what they say they want, the form of financial benefit they typically desire most is **long-term financial security**. This is one's ability to know that the money thing is mostly taken care of.

UNIQUE EXPERIENCES *(AND FRIENDSHIPS)*

Most people want to know what fringe **benefits** are offered when they consider a new position. The coveted perks most often mentioned are; benefits, trips, recognition and awards. It's all good, but the most phenomenal fringe benefit for us has been the memories that we've made, and the great friendships we've forged on the trips and in the trenches. It's a huge thing to be in sales and have companies lavish these great trips and awards on you. We've been able to go on more "vacations" than we've ever imagined. The running joke with Chuck's team is, "How many vacations will Ruthie (Chuck's wife) get to go on this year?" However, the one very special (and overlooked) element of this is the incredible blessing of being able to get to know our fellow sales professionals and their spouses on a personal basis. The time spent together often grows into life long relationships and close friendships. It's hard to place a price tag on that!

An Awesome Competitive Environment

Competition fuels certain people, and a large percentage of sales professionals fit into that demographic. Michael Jordan is famous for being ultra competitive, and not just on the basketball court. He gets fired up for a game of poker, golf, Ping-Pong or whatever the "game" is. Regardless of the game, he wants to win it. Competitors like to compete, and high-level commission sales is the ultimate game.

> *"Competitors like to compete, and high-level commission sales is the ultimate game."*

Our business is one that lends itself to this type of WINNING mindset. We can "WIN" today, this week, this quarter and this year. We can "WIN" in production, new clients, recruiting and customer service.

There are so many more reasons to do what we do. These are just a few to get your juices flowing. The key here is for you to dig deep inside of yourself and unquestionably recognize your WHYs. When things get a little tough, you can **employ a WHY**—you can use it like sailors use a lighthouse. You'll FOCUS on them and your energy will come flooding back, and you'll get back on a clear path to everything you've dreamed of achieving and being.

> *"You'll FOCUS on them and your energy will come flooding back..."*

We'll leave you with this one last thought from **John Gordon**:

> *"Remember WHY you do what you do. We don't get burned out (or lose our way) because of WHAT we do. We get burned out because we forget WHY we do it."*

CHAPTER 3

The Right Kind of Passion

What you wish to BUILD + BECOME

JOE BUZZELLO

*"It's hard to tell with some startups—if they're really interested in **building companies** or if they're just interested in money. I can tell you, though: If they don't really want to **BUILD** a business, they won't luck into it. That's because it's so hard that if you don't have a **passion** for **building** something, you'll give up."*

—STEVE JOBS

There are countless sales gurus, leadership authorities and motivational morons that scream from their platforms that you MUST have an **enormous passion** for what you do and sell—some implore you to focus on the outcome of money.

They're not 100% wrong. Passion for what you do and sell, and want-

15

ing to make a lot of money is fine, but their sound bites (in their simplest forms) can also de-rail people—cause them to focus on the wrong stuff—and then bail out early because they aren't feeling warm and fuzzy 24/7.

People have asked me the same few (similar) questions about PAS-SION for years now...

> *"Do you have to LOVE the products you're selling?"*
>
> *"Is it critical that you have a passion for ALL of the work that you do on a daily basis?"*
>
> *"Should I focus on the money—will that be enough to get me to my end goal?"*

Look...you may or may not be in LOVE with the products you're selling. You'd actually be lucky to wake up every morning with a fire in your belly for all of the work that you do.

If you only focus on the money, it may not be enough.

I sold employee benefits for many years, and although I was proud of what our products did in the lives of people, I can't honestly tell you that I "loved" the products themselves. The products were lifeless in and of themselves—completely inanimate. So I guess that I'd answer the first question with a shrug of the shoulders and a, "no." It's not a hard requirement that you love your products. I think you have to believe in them, I'm just not sure you have to have a massive love for them.

The second question, the one about having a passion for all of the **work** that you do on a daily basis...this one is a little trickier. First I'd ask you if you've ever known of a career, job or position whereby ALL of the prerequisite tasks each day were your **most favorite** work—you had 100% passion for everything required of you—no negatives—no downsides—no complaints?

Have you ever actually seen a gig like that?

Because I haven't!

Guess what...there are a number of **trade-offs** in every gig.

So the answer to that second question is also a "no"...you don't have to have a massive passion for ALL of the specific work. In fact you'll probably *dislike* some of the work involved in your sales career.

We'd like to get you thinking about the attitude you'll need to develop around the word PASSION, and more importantly, **what** your passion should be centered on.

Look, salespeople bring many flawed mindsets into their gigs, then their inventory of mindsets become even more unsound as they listen to some of the crap spewed out by motivational speakers or writers **that have never built anything**. They may get the impression that they'll need to have immense passion for all of the individual elements of their gig. This flaw in thinking will set them up for a rather quick failure, or even worse, a slow painful death in sales.

So rather than trying to find immense passion in your **product**, your daily **tasks**, the **company** you represent, or the **money** you'll make, we'd like to redirect your passion to something bigger, something easier to manage and something ultimately more sustainable.

> *"...We'd like to redirect your passion to something bigger, something easier to manage and something ultimately more sustainable."*

We want you to establish a mindset and **attitude** about **passion** that will set you up for long-term success. To that end, let's spend just a moment on what we'll call, the **right kind** of passion. In our experience, the right kind of passion is a hunger for the things that are less **shiny object** oriented and more fundamental in nature—more lasting.

WHAT YOU WISH TO BUILD

If you took note of the Steve Jobs quote at the top of this chapter, he was commenting on what happens when someone has a great idea for a business startup, but focuses on the wrong things. Jobs was suggesting that sometimes people launch new gigs and attach their passion to the outcome of big money. Mr. Jobs is suggesting that if people launch a business just to make bank, and they aren't really passionate about **building a business** (and be-coming something more in the process), they probably won't make it.

Jobs states that they won't, "luck into," any form of success. We know this is true because, building a legacy in your career is so hard that if you don't have a passion for the total **PROCESS**, you will probably quit! You'll give up before any measurable success occurs!

> *"...Building a legacy in your career is so hard that if you don't have a passion for the total PROCESS, you will probably quit! You'll give up before any measurable success occurs!*

We're challenging you to fall in love with the **process**—to direct your passion **there** versus anything less significant—and almost everything is **less** significant than the process of building a profitable business. We want a **profitable business** to be your **end product.** A stable business is the object that all of your passion should be focused on. If your passion is directed to this journey-related goal, then you'll never sweat the small stuff. You'll never even think about the work that you don't love. When things get tough, and the cash hasn't begun to flow yet, you won't quit. You'll have your eyes focused on something bigger.

> *"If your passion is directed to this journey-related goal, then you'll never sweat the small stuff."*

Let's go one other place before we end this chapter...

WHAT YOU WISH TO BECOME

We would like you to consider one more aspect of your journey—focus-ing on what you wish to **become** (personally and professionally) as you go about the work of building a business.

Beginning with my first month in commission sales (July of 1979), I had a great enthusiasm for personal and professional growth. It started with my agency director at Penn Life, Bud Cole. He challenged me to read the Napoleon Hill classic, *Think and Grow Rich*. I read that book until the pages fell out. I was blessed to have a natural enthusiasm for self-improvement—a hunger to grow—become better and smarter, every day. My enthusiasm for **becoming** something **more** was a huge reason that I became a self-made multi-millionaire at a rather young age.

> ## *"I was blessed to have a natural enthusiasm for self-improvement—a hunger to grow— become better and smarter, every day."*

Think about this. I was eighteen years old in 1979, just getting started in commission sales. I read a book. I got fired up and then I bought, borrowed or swiped any informational or motivational book or cassette tape I could get my hands on. The more I read and heard, the more I wanted to read and hear.

I guess I was **fortunate** enough to have **NOT** gone to college.

Let me explain...

Because I barely graduated high school, I had an **inferiority** complex— along with a few other insecurities. LOL! When I was in the presence of college graduates, I became rather uncomfortable. I knew that I needed to **catch up** to the "smartest people in the room." I had to figure out how to self-educate, and books, tapes, seminars and mentors were my path to accomplish that. I was a sponge, trying to become something more than a guy who barely survived high school. As my business and income grew, I didn't lag behind it from a professional growth perspective.

And oh...there's a form of growth that's equally important—**personal growth**. Personal growth is this intangible thing that many salespeople and wannabe entrepreneurs ignore completely. We find that some simply give lip service to personal growth. Bottom line, they don't have an established mindset about it, and that catches up to them.

Let me iterate on this...

Over the years we've seen many talented people that worked their tails off to build great careers in sales. As a result of their talent and hard work, they produced a great deal of income. However, we've also observed that some of these people couldn't maintain their success long term. We've seen lives come apart at the seams because of poor personal habits, addictions, morality issues, horrible professional relationships, failed marriages, poor spending habits, etc.

All of this carnage occurs when a person fails to grow **personally**.

Think about it...

If you're **not** striving to become a better person in all areas of your life (including your spiritual life) you can easily wake up one day to realize that your debts exceed your assets and it's bankruptcy time. Or, worse, you go to your mailbox and find a letter from the I.R.S. advising you that they've garnished your wages and cleaned out your bank accounts. You can arrive home one night and find that your spouse has packed up their stuff and moved out. Or you can become the unfortunate person that develops an out of control substance abuse problem or sex addiction.

I've been at this game (leading people) for over four decades. I've seen all of this and more. It's ugly to watch and also gut wrenching when you love people like I do. But this is what happens when people place all of their focus on the wrong things. If you develop a sincere passion for what you want to **build** and what you wish to **become** in that process, you'll grow in harmony with your income and accolades...and most likely, none of the bad crap we described will occur in your life.

So my hypothesis in this chapter is simple. If you place your focus and passion on the process of **building** a great business, and what you wish to **become** personally and professionally in that process, you'll be setting yourself up for a much better, happier and more purposeful life.

"If you place your focus and passion on the process of building a great business, and what you wish to become personally and professionally in that process, you'll be setting yourself up for a much better, happier and more purposeful life."

I have an intense passion for the process of building things. I also love the idea that I can grow personally and passionately every day. Do I love the products I choose to sell? Sure, but my products are more or less "tools" that enable me to build something bigger. Do I have a passion for all of the work it takes to build my business? Nah. I do like most of it, but some of the work sucks at times. However, I'm never focused on that. I'm not wasting my "passion" on those smaller things.

My passion is attached to the **right things**. I've always had the right kind of passion. I'm focused on what I want to BUILD and what I wish to BECOME in the process.

Little else matters.

And I don't let silly little things get in my way.

This mindset has made me millions and millions of dollars.

CHAPTER 4

A Big, Clear Vision

Getting this mindset right

JOE BUZZELLO

*"The two are not mutually exclusive, but we think
we can have wealth **without** a clear vision."*

—ANDREW YOUNG

So I'm in a barbecue joint in Northridge, California. It's 1998. I have a new territory director sitting in front of me. She's asking about WHERE I plan to, "take" my organization. Specifically, she wanted to know **when** I thought I could hit the ten million dollar mark in annual production. I loosely guaranteed her that I could, "Get us there in four or five years."

Wrong answer!

As soon as I said it I knew it wasn't what she wanted to hear. The look of contempt on her face was both humorous and scary. I won't bore you with the rant that she peeled off into, but it was quite entertaining. Bottom line—she pushed back hard.

She challenged both the **size** and **clarity** of my vision.

I wasn't a rookie at the art of placating the new home office honkie. I'd been in sales and leadership for twenty years at this juncture. I knew what to tell these folks to make them feel good. The goal was to get them to buy me a beer, and then point them back to the ivory tower from whence they came.

I was a hard-core pro.

The only problem I had was that I was sitting across the table from a **harder**-core pro. And she wasn't gonna' let me off the hook. As she pushed back, reminding me of the huge population base in my territory, I slumped in my chair. She was scribbling out metrics on a yellow pad with a red pen—showing me how we could reach the ten million dollar mark within two years. The red ink and barbecue sauce mixed together made our table look like a crime scene—and the crime in her eyes was my **less than compelling** vision. It was obvious to me that she wasn't going to back off.

Please understand that (at the time of this meeting) our team was barely annualizing at five million and I'd built that base of production from scratch in just over five years. It had taken a lot of blood, sweat and tears to get to five mil. My logic was that it would take another five years to get to ten million.

She asked me a question:

> *"Joe, if it WAS possible to hit ten million inside of two years, what would it take—what would you have to CHANGE about yourself and your organization?"*

Great question.

In fact, a **brilliant** question.

I took a swig out of the frosty Corona bottle that had magically appeared in front of me, and I took my time answering. I'd quickly figured out that my newly assigned territory director didn't suffer foolish answers well. I began to earnestly think about **what it would take** to go from five to ten million in two years. I contemplated the changes I'd have to make inside of my business, both structurally and culturally. A few logical moves came to mind—ones that would take guts to make and might be painful. I then reflected on what changes I'd have to make **inside of my own head** and ONE thing in particular rose to the top of my mind.

I would need to start thinking **BIG** again—I'd need to get out there on that long imaginary limb.

> ### *"I would need to start thinking BIG again—I'd need to get out there on that long imaginary limb."*

It wasn't that I didn't have an established mindset about vision being critically important. I implored all of our new salespeople to have seeds of faith, a vision of what they wished to build and become and then get to work watering those seeds—doing the work.

I certainly had a vision!

It simply wasn't **BIG** or **clear** enough at that particular juncture.

We're going to commit the rest of this chapter to how you can develop a BIG vision and also make it crystal clear. But first I want to make sure you have completely bought into the importance of a BIG, clear vision and you know WHAT it is and WHY it's so important to have the right mindset surrounding your vision.

WHAT IS A BUSINESS VISION?

Vision is a **mental picture**—a sense of what the future holds for you. Your vision is merely an **affirmation** of your long-term objectives. It **guides** your thoughts and actions. Your vision should generate a desire to get better. It symbolizes your **hopes** and **ideals** and gives you a sense of purpose. Vision delivers a glimpse of what's possible.

It enables us to look AHEAD and avert catastrophe before it happens, or plan for increases in staffing, production, etc. Vision helps a leader prepare for the future. Vision keeps a leader on course during rocky times or unexpected setbacks. Having a plan for success in your business is one of the most valuable things you can have.

Vision provides **MOTIVATION** *that inspires us to keep going.* Leaders need to keep the end result in mind. A leader's vision needs to be strong enough to carry them through to the end. If you have a BIG and clear vision, then setbacks will seem small or insignificant. You'll work through the obstacles and get to the finish line—learning as you go. Vision helps people persevere.

Vision provides **FOCUS.** With all of the white noise and all the people vying for our attention, it can be hard to feel a sense of accomplishment. Acting on your vision will provide you with the focus needed to accomplish your goals. Vision helps leaders work on what's important to achieve the end results and not get caught up in the mundane stuff. It helps leaders to focus on the 20% that is important instead of the remaining 80% that can be delegated and handled by others.

Vision gives us meaning and **PURPOSE.** It will help you to see the end result of your efforts. It will give you your "why" and the reason that you're doing what you do.

DEVELOP A BIG, CLEAR VISION-BASED MINDSET

Begin with a VISION STATEMENT (for you or your team)

Begin formulating your vision statement by asking the following **questions**:

- Where do I see myself/my business in 2 – 5 years? (Beam yourself into the future!)
- *What does it look like if my business is* **competing well** *in (or dominating) the market?*

Continue by EXPANDING your mindset *(Your vision should live in a world with limitless possibilities)*

- *What would it take to **double my revenue** (or income) in 5 years?*
- *Should I operate in **different geographic** areas?*
- *Would it be wise to add **different** (or additional) **products** or services to my arsenal?*
- *Should I seek out **strategic partnerships**?*

Ask a few questions about your current/future POSITIONING

Consider your company type, structure and position as you formulate your big vision:

- *How does my company's POSITION **speak** to the vision?*
- *Why does my business **exist**?*
- *How do I do things **differently**, better, or more efficiently?*
- *What sets me/us **apart**?*

Hopefully, we've shed some light on the what, why and how that goes into the **creation** of your big, clear vision. Bottom line, we want you to get down and dirty answering the following six **golden** questions:

- *What is the **ideal world** that I aim to build?*
- *How **CLEAR** can I formulate my vision? (In my mind and on paper)*
- *How **fast** can I build this business?*
- *What **resources** will I need to get the job done?*
- *What will I have to **become** in the process?*
- *How **large** can I scale my business if <u>anything</u> is possible?*

I believe that these six questions (if asked and answered honestly) hold the key to you growing your business to massive size and strength. It's 100% true that we will NOT develop great wealth without a **BIG** and **CLEAR** vision. It simply isn't going to happen.

So now back to my story—1998—that barbecue place in Northridge, CA.

My new territory V.P. had challenged me to think about my business on a **grander** scale and she coaxed me into *sharpening up* the picture.

(What it would take and what it would look like) She dared me to **double** my business ("get to ten million") in just two years. Originally, I thought this would be impossible—that it couldn't happen—that it would take much longer than that.

Ultimately, I was right.

It did take longer.

We didn't get to ten million in two years.

However, we were annualizing at that number **in just two years and eight months**...well ahead of the five-year pace that I'd established in my mind. Before my new territory director challenged me, I was simply thinking too small and the picture in my head wasn't quite vibrant enough.

I simply **adjusted** those two things and wealth followed.

Okay...

Can you begin to dream a little bigger? Can you conjure up a crystal clear image of what you wish to build and become?

Your turn.

Go!

CHAPTER 5

The Other Side of "WHY"

Developing an attitude of understanding + empathy

Leon Davidson with Joe Buzzello

*"When you show deep empathy toward others, their **defensive energy** goes down, and positive energy replaces it"*

—Stephen Covey

Before we leave the word "WHY" alone, we're going to look at one more facet of it.

Simon Sinek, the well-known British-American author and motivational speaker, has inspired many people with the book *"Start With Why"*. He has also received countless accolades for his Ted Talks on the subject.

Sinek challenges us to examine the reason people buy from someone like you. His hypothesis is that it's all about "your why". He states:

"People don't buy WHAT you do, they buy WHY you do it".

He proposes that people will buy from you if you get them to understand WHY you believe in something.

This makes sense.

For example, think about the last time you made a large purchase, such as a car. Your decision may have had something to do with the way the dealership; showroom and salesperson made you **feel**. They wanted you to feel a certain way so that you would identify with **their** "why". If you *felt* and **understood** their passion, you'd want to buy one of their cars from them.

But like most things in life, there's another **side** of things. In this chapter we'll examine the WHY from the viewpoint of the **buyer**. We'll encourage you to develop an attitude of understanding + empathy so that you can discover **THEIR** why.

Let's go back to the example of buying a car. The fact is, you probably wouldn't walk into a car dealership if you didn't have a **purpose**. Perhaps, your car just conked out. Maybe you drove it until it had three hundred thousand miles on it, and it's time to part with it. Perhaps you were interested in buying a car for a son or daughter. You're there at the dealership for the same reason (to buy a car), but not for the same purpose.

If you're purchasing a car for yourself, your "why" may be centered on a long-term investment in comfort, luxury and personal transportation. However, the "why" connected with a purchase for your son or daughter may have more to do with the safety features of the vehicle. Hence, whichever salesperson best **identifies your real purpose**, and then proves to you that their "why" and yours are in sync, gets the win.

"...Whichever salesperson best identifies your real purpose, and then proves to you that their "why" and yours are in sync, gets the win."

In practice, the salesperson who's able to understand your "why", and provide you with the **feeling** that you're getting **exactly** what you want, gets the deal.

We think that you may be familiar with the **six basic questions** used in information gathering:

- WHO
- WHAT
- WHEN
- WHERE
- WHY
- + HOW

We hope that you have been trained to use these key adverbs in your engagement and discovery process. All of these words (and the questions you form around them) are designed to help you **reach into the mind** of the person you're presenting your products to. You've hopefully been taught to learn about your prospect's needs, wants, etc. This is all good and necessary, but we'd like you to go just a little bit **deeper**. We'd like you to develop a core attitude of **understanding** and **empathy** so that when you're sitting face-to-face with your prospect, something more than flat-line questions are used to engage them.

If you aren't sure what **empathy** really means, it is the ability to **understand and share the feelings** of another person. We're challenging you to develop a mindset that enables you to sense other people's emotions. We'd like you to imagine what someone else may be thinking or feeling in the moment.

> *"We're challenging you to develop a mindset that enables you to sense other people's emotions. We'd like you to ask questions to discover what someone else may be thinking or feeling in the moment."*

This mindset and attitude of empathy makes it possible for you to truly understand what they believe, think and feel, which will form the basis of their buying decisions.

Let's look at one more illustration of how this works...

Suppose you sell life insurance and you've been invited to meet with two partners of a business. During the initial phone call they told you that they're interested in purchasing life insurance. It would be typical for a new salesperson to walk into their office, guns blazing, and data dump on the two partners about why the company they represent is the best, and describe how different types of life insurance plans work. The proto-typical salesperson continues to throw out useless facts—biggest, oldest, cheapest, blah, blah, blah.

Who knows, this dude may even make a sale.

But, he missed a **golden** opportunity!

The salesperson in this example missed the chance to practice real empathy and understanding. He blew the chance to discover the prospect's **core motivations**. If the same salesperson walked into the door with an attitude of understanding and empathy, he would have begun to ask thoughtful questions regarding their current position. If he were practic-ing genuine empathy he would ask questions in a very **different way** than the typical salesperson. The questions would come across as **caring**, and when this happens, another thing happens, their **defensive walls** come down and positive energy fills the room.

This is a good thing, right?

When you're focused on finding out about their "why", you will dis-cover all of the underlying (unspoken) motivations and reasons they felt that your product would benefit them. This level of conversation can (and usually does) change their perception of you. You become **LESS a sales-person** or vendor, and you move closer to becoming a **trusted advisor**, which affords you so many more opportunities to help them.

EXAMPLES OF EMPATHETIC QUESTIONS

Let's demonstrate how the adverbs we're referring to can be used by a salesperson who's developing an empathetic attitude. Here are a few sample questions:

- *Why did you folks call me?*
- *What are you hoping to learn today?*
- *Who else do you plan to talk to about these needs?*
- *I'm curious, why do you feel our product may be the right answer?*
- *Why do you feel that this is the right time to look into our services?*

Of course, we can easily expand the list of questions, however, from just these five questions, you could uncover many answers, such as...

What they perceive about you—your company
What KEY answers they want to take away from the meeting
Who your competition may be
What they know (or think they know) about your company or product
What's the underlying reason for the purchase—is it a business or personal issue
What their timeline for a purchase may be

More importantly than simply learning about these triggers, if you're coming from a genuine place of empathy, you'll learn how you can make a real difference in the lives of the people you're selling to. When you consciously position yourself in this way, it becomes obvious to them that you are on their side. You'll not only consummate a sale, you'll have a valued client relationship for life.

> *"When you consciously position yourself in this way, it becomes obvious to them that you are on their side. You'll not only consummate a sale, you'll have a valued client relationship for life."*

So this is **the other side of the "why"** and why it's so important to establish an attitude of understanding and empathy. We certainly all have our **OWN** "why". It defines who we are, and why we are doing what we do, but our ability to successfully discover their "why" (and then aligning our "why' with theirs), is our road to sustained success...

...and a much HIGHER closing ratio! ☺

Section 2

Faith, Confidence, Commitment + Determination

*How faith **works**, the importance of confidence and **POISE** during the journey, and your ability to victoriously **FINISH** the race that you started.*

CHAPTER 6

Small Seeds of Faith

*The seeds are there...you simply
need to water them*

JOE BUZZELLO

*"Though I do not believe that a plant will spring up where **no
seed** has been, I have great **faith** in a seed... Convince me that
you have a seed there, and I am prepared to expect wonders."*

—HENRY DAVID THOREAU

Faith is a funny thing.

Us coaches ***throw*** this word around a lot.

Maybe too much.

In this chapter I'm going to challenge you to take another look at this important word and position it as a mindset, then **connect it** directly to your ultimate success.

There was a specific time in my life when the only **true currency** I had was faith. Between March of 1987 and October of 1988 I slowly—but surely—lost almost everything that was important to me. I don't like to dwell on the past, but for the sake of context I will list the gut punches I absorbed:

I lost...

- All of my money and assets
- Most of my family's retirement savings
- My business
- My confidence *(and ability to trust people)*
- My good reputation
- My supposed best friend *(and all of my business relationships)*
- My good credit rating *(I filed personal bankruptcy)*
- My marriage *(My wife walked out)*
- My father *(from lung cancer)*
- My ability to get out of bed in the morning

I hadn't reached the age of twenty-seven and my world had come crashing down around me.

Completely.

As I sat on my old couch—one of the few pieces of furniture that had not been repossessed or sold—I finished the box of bad red wine and then polished off a handle of Jack.

It was a Saturday night, October 15th 1988.

I'd just finished watching an epic Dodger game. Hard-core baseball fans may recognize the October date. It was game one of the 1988 World Series—the game where Kirk Gibson hit his heroic home run. Vin Scully's call was a classic. As the ball sailed over the right field wall Vinny wailed, "She is gone." Then he went silent for approximately one minute and ten seconds. He let the events on the screen tell the story and he permitted the emotions of the players and fans to wash over the viewers. After more than a minute of silence, Scully said:

"In a year that has been so improbable, the impossible has happened."

Tears streamed down my face as I got up and turned off the TV. I wasn't sure why I was crying.

I'm not sure even today.

Maybe it was because Vin Scully's call of the Dodgers "impossible" win had just carried me back to my childhood—everything that I loved when I was a kid, listening to Vin Scully's voice on my transistor radio in the bedroom I grew up in. Maybe I was crying because I'd made such a mess out of my life.

The big home in Woodland Hills, California—the one in its third month of foreclosure—was cold and lonely. I lit a fire in the fireplace. I found one more half empty bottle of hard liquor—don't ask me what it was...I think it was Old Grand Dad. I sipped on the bottle like it was a twelve-ounce beer. I staggered into my office and began to collect every sales award that I'd earned to that point in my career—and there were plenty of them. I grabbed the ones I knew would burn.

I'd kill two birds with one stone.

I'd warm up the house and also **erase** my prior professional life.

The fire raged as I slipped into an alcohol-induced coma. I awoke around six in the morning. The smoke alarms were ear piercing and the living room featured a layer of smoke that looked like a San Fernando Valley smog blanket. Steams of smoke rose from the brown carpet. Hot embers still burned bright inside the fireplace and my oak mantle had been partially destroyed by the flames that escaped the confines of the fireplace. To this day, I'm still not certain how I didn't burn my entire house down to the ground that night. It's also not logical that I didn't succumb to smoke inhalation in my sleep.

I swayed to my feet and opened every door and window and poured water on the hot spots that were still smoldering on the carpet. When I sat back down I realized that I had tried to kill myself the previous night. I'd done my best to burn my life down. Perhaps it wasn't completely intentional, but then again, maybe it was.

As I began to sober up, I prayed.

I hadn't prayed in a long time.

For the sake of brevity, it isn't important HOW I'd managed to lose almost everything over the previous year. If you're curious, read my second book, Drawing Circles. Let's just conclude that I'd made a disaster of my life by making poor choices. Then I had some bad luck, followed by MORE bad luck, followed by a few more bad decisions.

My prayer was simple.

> *"God, please give me the strength to start over and make things right. I want to honor You and make my mother and departed father proud of what I can become. I want to start over and do things right."*

I recall the prayer because I prayed it for a solid month after that incident. But on that Sunday morning I just cleaned up my mess, swallowed four Tylenol, drank some warm orange juice and I sobered up. I sat on the couch for quite a while that day, just thinking about my life. It wasn't like I had anything to do or anyone to do it with. I reflected on all that I had lost—had a small pity party. After praying again my thoughts shifted towards all of the things that I had NOT lost.

I recall taking an inventory.

I still had...

- My health
- My wonderful mother, sister, aunt and family
- A few close friends
- My knowledge of sales and a love of coaching and training
- My desire to lead and influence people

- A killer work ethic
- My sense of humor
- A faith in God
- Some small seeds of faith

That word.

FAITH.

It kept creeping into my thought process. I thought about how I could strengthen my faith in God. Then I began to assess the level of faith I had in myself and it occurred to me that I had a hell of a lot more faith in God's ability at that juncture than I had in mine.

But I was hanging onto those **small seeds of faith**.

I began to think about how I could start over, what it would take and how it would feel. I allowed myself to dream a little. I also went into my office and grabbed my dictionary. Since that word wouldn't leave my head, **I looked faith up**. The definition states that faith is:

"complete trust or confidence in someone or something"

I knew that. I also knew that seeds of faith exist **before** there is any **proof** or evidence. I read the definition over again, asking myself, do you really have **complete** trust or confidence in yourself right now?

The truth was...I didn't.

I didn't have anywhere near a "complete" level of faith. But I did have those small seeds. I did believe that it was possible for me to dust myself off and **go back to work** again. My faith in my ability to sell—and teach others to sell was still there.

"I did believe that it was possible for me to dust myself off and go back to work again."

I won't bore you with the details of my journey back, but that afternoon was the genesis of it. I latched onto those small slivers of faith and simply made the decision to take my head out of my butt and **go back to work**.

As I sat on my couch in that smoky living room I thought again about Vin Scully's call of Kirk Gibson's home run the previous night.

"In a year that has been so improbable, the impossible has happened."

It had surely been an **improbable** year for me.

How was I to know that I would suffer the incredible tsunami of crap that would include my father's sudden passing from cancer, the betrayal of so many people that were close to me, the complete destruction of my finances and my wife walking out—leaving me emotionally devastated.

An **improbable** year for me...for sure.

The **impossible** part of this scenario may not be as obvious.

As I reflect on that day in particular, it doesn't seem that plausible that someone in my condition should have a **sudden awakening of faith**. It had to be a God thing. He just wasn't done with me yet, or something like that.

Fast-forward almost a decade...

I'm at the bar at Dodgertown, Vero Beach, Florida. It's 1997 MLB spring training. I'm remarried to this beautiful lady named Beth. We are VIP guests of the L.A. television station (KTLA) that broadcasted the Dodgers at that time. I was well into the process of building what would become a hundred million dollar insurance agency. This awesome team would also become a legacy sales organization for the Fortune 500' company that I worked with. I recall how happy I was that weekend in Vero Beach. I'd nurtured those small seeds of faith that were planted inside me almost ten years earlier. My life had become something that I could be proud of.

As if on cue, Vin Scully walks into the bar.

I introduced myself to him and mentioned that I was on his 1969 NBC game show, *It Takes Two*, when I was eight years old. He laughs and said, *"Get out of here...nobody remembers that old show."* I told him that his call of Kirk's famous home run—almost ten years earlier—had brought tears to my eyes. I described it to him as a lone joyous moment during the lowest point of my life. Vin smiled—he didn't say anything—he simply reached over and clinked my beer mug with his scotch glass.

He seemed to understand.

The following ten years were even better for me, bringing Beth and I a beautiful daughter named, Alyssa, and even more success and happiness.

It all started with those small seeds of faith.

I'm convinced that God planted those seeds and after that, it was up to me to pour water on them. I did that by identifying what I had NOT lost. It was **ON** me to use the gifts and talents that I'd been given. It's my belief that having faith—even when there's no evidence that you'll do something great—is a far more **potent** attitude than almost any other.

> *"It's my belief that having faith—even when there's no evidence that you'll do something great—is a far more potent attitude than almost any other."*

God planted those **small seeds of faith** inside of me on that Sunday morning in October of 1988. I'm so glad that I was smart enough to water and nurture those seeds over the next thirty years.

Your seeds are there...inside of you.

You simply need to identify them and water them.

CHAPTER 7

Positioning Faith As a Verb

Negotiating the "mind mines"
through action

DAWN TYACK WITH JOE BUZZELLO

*"Is a faith without **action** a sincere faith?"*

—JEAN RACINE

Bill had diligently planned for this moment. He did all of the research to make a solid decision. He saved his money, and negotiated the best deal possible on his new truck. It was beautiful—all he had hoped for, a V8, 4x4, mud flaps and a front bumper winch. It was fully loaded and ready for the big adventure.

With great expectations, he jumped into the truck ready for the trip that lay ahead. Bill loaded up his truck with all of the necessary gear and headed out knowing his brand new vehicle was equipped to take him off the main road, and onto the road less traveled. Tunes blasted from the dashboard as he took in the rugged scenery and visualized how his new pickup was going to impact his life in the years to come. After all, it was so much better than the old junker he had just traded in.

Bill turned off the main road into the backcountry that he so loved to trek. Bouncing along the rough road, a broad smile brimmed across his face. Soon the road grew so narrow that it disappeared into a tangle of weeds, shrubs and big rocks. The path became a bit muddy, but no problem, the new truck moved along easily.

What fun!

As he crossed over the creek and into the meadow, Bill noticed that the ground had become much softer and trickier. He threw the truck into 4-wheel drive. He chugged along until his tires sunk into a bog that was concealed beneath some tall grasses. His truck tires began to spin. He stepped on the gas hard, but the tires just spun, kicking a ton of mud into the air. Bill was still poised. He believed the new, powerful truck would pull him through. After all, it was the perfect vehicle for this kind of situation. He had faith in the vehicle. But as he hit the quicksand-like bog, his wheels dug deeper and deeper. He began to lose some of that faith he started with.

He begins to sweat and has his fingers on the mobile phone...maybe this trip to the backcountry was a mistake, he thinks. Perhaps I should call a tow truck—just quit this journey and turn back for home.

Bill's faith is being **tested**, big time

Have you ever felt like your wheels are spinning in the mud—a bit stuck—and your faith was being tested?

We're quite sure that you started your sales career with the best intentions—to be productive and super successful. But like Bill's experience, sometimes it feels like everything is falling apart. You feel like you can't get anything accomplished. Appointments cancel, sales opportunities are pushing back or postponing. You aren't hitting your numbers and everyone expects much more out of you—and truthfully, you expected more of yourself.

You think, "Maybe I should quit...do something else. Maybe I should give up on this dream and this career—go get a real job." This is like Bill's experience in the muddy bog. We call this a case of the **"Mind Mines"**.

So let's go back to that pristine place that you started at. Just like Bill's new truck, you didn't have a scratch or even a spot of mud on you. You got underway cleanly with mounds of faith—faith in your abilities, your product, the process, etc. You "drank the Kool-Aid" and you were a believer!

It's all good.

We all start there.

But faith is merely a **NOUN** at the inception of your journey.

It isn't anything tangible until it is put into action, then it becomes a **VERB**. And the attitude and mindset of positioning faith as a verb becomes the most foundational element of your eventual success.

> ### *"...The attitude and mindset of positioning faith as a verb becomes the most foundational element of your eventual success."*

Faith has to be **tested**.

It has to transition from a NOUN to a VERB—it has to become an **act**.

It has to be tested—otherwise you can't refer to it as faith. Faith is not only your belief in things not yet seen (noun), but more importantly, it is **the actions you take** based on your faith. A fruitful sales or entrepreneurial career must consist of faith "the **noun**" and faith "the **verb**."

We believe that faith (when you apply it to a sales or entrepreneurial career) should be:

- *At the **core** of why you decide to do what you do*
- *Your ultimate **WHY**.*
- *Your internal **compass***

- *Your **conviction***

So all of the sales legends step out in faith to begin their career. They all began at that same place. Everything was going along as planned. The birds were chirping and they were filled with excitement and anticipation on their newfound path.

Then along came the marshy, swampy, hidden bog...or as we call them, the "mind mines." (This happens to every one of us) We find ourselves lost in an avalanche of mental crap. Too much to do—too paralyzed to take another step, or we aren't sure what the next step even is. We can't seem to get our thoughts to gather into anything that resembles a logical or tangible strategy.

The mind mines are taking over and we are then presented with a big choice...

...turn back, *or take* massive action.

I think you know what sales and entrepreneurial legends do, right? They **push through** the swampy mess and get to the other side. They accomplish this by putting their faith into something that resembles massive action. All of the killer hard-core sales pros and entrepreneurs that we know are constantly at work on the further development of their attitude of faith. We want you to get a better feel for what top income earners **think** and **do** in this area, so here are **5 methods** that we know work 100% of the time to drive higher levels of faith and action:

5 Methods Pros Use to Position Faith as ACTION

Turn off the WHITE NOISE

If their minds are **crowded** with junk, top performers begin to eliminate all of the white noise that may find their ears and eyes. They turn off the **news** and turn on their **muse**. Work to eliminate all unessential forms of input that are not supporting your mission and vision. Clear away the junk in your head.

Don't engage in any NEGATIVITY

When a conversation with loved ones, peers or friends begins to veer toward anything negative, the great ones simply stop the conversation. Just excuse yourself and walk away. We all have people in our lives who can gossip or get negative. Sometimes the best option is to just walk away from the conversation. Your faith needs **nurturing** and negative stuff doesn't achieve that objective.

Monitor your Inner *(and outer)* VOICE

A big part of faith is being patient and monitoring your self-talk and comments. Top performers take time to think about their thoughts. They also *think* before they *speak* instead of just blurting out whatever comes into their head. This makes a huge difference as you employ your faith and turn it into action.

ORGANIZE your MIND *(and calendar)*

When your mind and calendar are a mess, and you have a million things on your to-do list, you can get super stressed out. Keep yourself on target by identifying your true business **priorities**. Recognize what **moves the needle** for your business. Focus on those things and put those things **in the calendar FIRST**.

Take MASSIVE ACTION

You knew this was coming, right? Take notice of the best of the best in our business, they have a **solid weekly action plan** and they **don't STRAY** from that plan of action.

> *"...The best of the best in our business have a solid weekly action plan and they don't STRAY from that plan of action."*

We'd like to wrap up this chapter by making sure that you totally get this point we are driving.

Faith is a **VERB**.

It's not a real thing until it gets **tested**.

And when it gets tested you must take **massive action**.

The good news is that great things usually seem to happen when you are taking action. When you stop to lick your wounds, or engage with negative people, or you begin to complain or your calendar is a mess...bad things happen.

Oh...and about Bill and his truck...

Bill got his head out of his rear end. He stopped spinning his tires in the mud, and cussing and feeling sorry for himself. He exercised some faith that he would figure things out. He got out of the truck, put his floodlights on and found some rocks and wood to create traction. He slowly backed out of the swamp and took a slightly different path to this campground destination.

He took some action—he re-positioned his faith as a VERB. Bill negotiated around all of the land mines and "mind mines" through his actions. Oh...and he got all muddy...and boy was he tired after the job was over, but he wound up having a great trip.

CHAPTER 8

Eagle-to-Eagle

Arriving at the table confidently

SCOTT STORJOHANN WITH JOE BUZZELLO

"If people like you, they'll listen to you, but if they
trust you, they'll do business with you."

—ZIG ZIGLAR

Is confidence **teachable**?

You may be less naturally confident than others, however, that doesn't mean you can't increase your confidence level significantly. If you Google search, "confidence", you'll see umpteen titles and find hundreds of videos on the subject. So it must be teachable, right? While we believe that building your level of confidence is possible, we also think it's tricky. We've seen countless theories on how people can position themselves to be perceived as "more confident", but we believe much of this is a Band-Aid for the **real thing**.

The real thing is what we call becoming, "Eagle-to-Eagle"

In short, this means being able to **match** strength against strength—being able to look your prospect straight in the eyeballs—positioning yourself on the same level while you engage.

How important is this thing we call Eagle-to-Eagle? We know it's **critical** in a selling situation. High-level decision-makers can literally **smell the fear** on a person who's scared or feels inferior to them. The truth is, decision makers don't give their business to weak, frightened or apprehensive salespeople. They want to award their business to strong, poised business people who are just like them, and that's what this chapter is about.

> *"...Decision makers don't give their business to weak, frightened or apprehensive salespeople. They want to award their business to strong, poised business people who are just like them."*

We want to advise you on a mindset that allows you to go Eagle-to-Eagle with each and every prospect you come in contact with. We believe that the development of this sort of true and **sustained confidence** must be attained in two of the distinct categories found inside of The CAP Equation—**Competencies** and/or **Attitudes**.

We believe that trying to develop an attitude of confidence that comes from a **manufactured** mindset, or working on confidence **only** from the perspective of your competencies, won't work. We contend that your ability to be truly confident in front of a prospect is a learned behavior that stems from a set of great core competencies and the adoption of specific outlooks—a total product of doing and thinking certain things.

Let's go back to this **"Eagle-to-Eagle"** thing for a moment.

The **position** we're suggesting you *adopt* as you walk in the door should be one of **equal ground**. We're suggesting that decision makers are similar to strong, confident birds of prey, ones that are searching for your soft white underbelly. These people have the ability to look right through you—to keenly observe your **potency**.

These people WANT to do business with **other eagles**.

Not chickens!

> *"...Decision makers are similar to strong, confident birds of prey, ones that are searching for your soft white underbelly."*

We've made several trips around the sun and we've seen it all regarding levels of confidence. (Or weakness) In Joe's third book, **A Life in Sales**, Volume 1, he writes about a young man that was so nervous about giving his first presentation that he vomited. While this may seem like a severe reaction to something as simple as presenting to a prospect, being scared or nervous is quite common. In fact, even the most seasoned sales pros have **butterflies** in their stomach before an important pitch. It's just that the pros know how to get their butterflies flying in formation!

> *"...Even the most seasoned sales pros have butterflies in their stomach before an important pitch. It's just that the pros know how to get their butterflies flying in formation!"*

To be able to go the distance in the sales game, you must learn how to control your butterflies and *mirror* your prospect's level of strength. The definition of confidence found in the dictionary suggests that...

> *"Confidence is a feeling of self-assurance arising from one's appreciation of one's own abilities and qualities."*

I like this definition because it addresses our tangible abilities as well as our intangible qualities.

Anna's Challenge

Allow us to give you an example of what can happen when you begin to think that your prospect is **more important** than you are. What I'm describing here is when a new (or even veteran) salesperson places themselves in a **subservient position** from the inception of the relationship.

We'll call her, "Anna." (Not her real name)

Anna entered the game of commission B2B sales with account service experience, but no real knowledge of outside sales. She was a good student—she learned a great deal about our products, how to present them, and how to ask for the sale. Her closing ratio wasn't awesome—there were far too many "maybes"—but nonetheless, at the six-month mark she had developed a decent block of business.

As she slogged through the second half of her year it became apparent to Anna's direct manager that her book of business was strangling her. The level of service she offered was above our standard practices (which is fine), however, we learned that her account contacts were calling her at all hours of the day. She was being run ragged—operating outside an acceptable scope of work—doing things she wasn't being paid to do.

Of course, her new account production slowed and then stopped completely. Worse, she was beginning to **hate** the business. It was at this juncture that Anna's direct manager and I dug into the situation to try to fix it. She was a valuable salesperson with a potentially great career ahead of her. When we started to ask questions, it became apparent that four interesting dynamics were in play:

1. *Anna had closed most of her sales with 2nd and 3rd level contacts (Someone other than the top decision maker/owner)*
2. *She'd developed little if any **connection** (or relationship) with the primary decision makers of her accounts*
3. *Anna had established herself as a **subservient** to her account*
4. *Her accounts were taking as **MUCH advantage** of her as possible (As much as she would allow)*

You get what happened here?

Anna had certainly become a competent salesperson, but she had failed to go **Eagle-to-Eagle** with the top decision makers of her accounts. She relegated herself to second or third tier personnel, forging no relationships at higher levels. Worse, Anna settled for the role of **servant**, rather than **equal**. The consequence of that is obvious. The underlings got a whiff of Anna's willingness to play the subservient role and they *pounced* on it.

And she was getting tired.

And she stopped producing new sales.

As she finished her first year, Anna realized that she didn't know how to approach top decision makers. As we dug deeper we learned that much of the problem stemmed from Anna's scripting. Anna suffered from a low self-image. To some degree we all suffer from this at times, however, Anna experienced a **fear** of people in powerful roles—people like business owners and executives. When she was in their presence, she'd immediately place herself as a subservient party. She'd call them, "Sir," or "Mrs.". Her body language changed when she was in front of a decision maker, her level of confidence, strength and conviction immediately shrunk. When Anna actually got an audience with a top tier decision maker, they'd talk to her for a moment, smell her weakness, and **pass her off** to an underling.

This isn't the path we want you to take in your sales career!

CREATING THE EAGLE-TO-EAGLE MINDSET!

Let's take a look at the philosophies, tactics and methods hard-core sales PROs employ to develop their Eagle-to-Eagle mindset.

Overall Mindsets:

Here's a list of 4 mindsets that great salespeople develop and apply:

- They view themselves as a **business owner** also. Even if you are an "intrapreneur" *(working inside an organizational structure as a 1099 rep.),* you must adopt the attitude that **YOU OWN** your own business.

- Top producers believe *(going in)* that they **know more** about their specific product or service than their prospect does.
- They *(100%)* believe that they can **be of VALUE** to the person they're sitting in front of.
- Great salespeople have an incredible amount of faith in their ability to identify and **solve future problems** for their clients and eventually become a **trusted advisor**.

Bottom line, the great ones go into every client meeting having adopted these attitudes—ones that serve them well as they position themselves **Eagle-to-Eagle** with their prospects and clients.

We would like to stress that everything we're talking about takes a great deal of practice. In Joe's first book, The Cap Equation, he introduces the acronym, "PDR." This stands for **Practice, Drill + Rehearse.** You can role-play the word text that positions you as an equal to the point that it becomes **second nature**, hence, your level of confidence will rise dramatically.

Have you actually listened to how you sound recently?

Scott likes to **record** and **listen to** parts of his business owner and/or employee presentations. He'll listen to these recordings the night before a big pitch or on his way to the appointment. As a result he doesn't have to think too hard about some of his key statements and questions when he's in front of his prospect or client. He has the key areas of his presentation wired—like he's singing along to his favorite song on the radio.

Think about that analogy. If you're listening to a popular song—one you've heard a few zillion times—it gets "stuck" in your head. Before you know it, you're nailing it—reciting each lyric in perfect timing to the recording.

That's the goal behind recording your perfect presentation.

This kind of PDR makes it possible for you to walk in and be eagle-to-eagle. It makes it possible for you to **develop GENUINE confidence** because you absolutely (100%) **KNOW** what you are going to ask and say. This sense of cool brings you onto a **level playing field** with your client.

They will view you as an equal because they will perceive that you know your stuff and they can trust you to make their life a little easier.

> *"You are having a positive and FLUID conversation. This sense of cool brings you onto a level playing field with your client."*

For over four decades, Joe has been saying, **"Competence breeds confidence."** Sometimes the reason salespeople don't take action is because they lack confidence. By carefully reviewing and applying the elements we have introduced you to in this chapter, we are sure you will improve your short-term results dramatically. More importantly, long-term, you'll develop the ability to walk through any door with your shoulders up, head held high—full of confidence.

Oops...we almost forgot about Anna!

Anna's immediate report (and Joe) were able to get into Anna's head. (And heart) Anna was quite coachable, mostly because she had hit an emotional rock bottom. LOL! Anna's coaches were able to help her remodel her approach to prospecting, closing and offering service.

The primary shift was in Anna's **attitudes.** She acknowledged that getting eagle-to-eagle with top decision makers was key to building the type of business she wanted. Of course, Anna had to be willing to **lose** a few clients, however, over the period of six to eight months she was able to add back the RIGHT kind of clients. She built a very strong block of business and experienced a phenomenally successful career that has endured for over two decades. Anna decided to become an eagle and then get eagle-to-eagle with high-level decision makers.

We want to reiterate one final thought before we put this chapter to bed.

How you perceive your professional stature, and how you **POSITION** yourself with your prospects is critical to your survival as a salesperson. When the decision maker you want to work with views you as a strategic partner and trusted advisor, then you've truly become an **Eagle-to-Eagle** pro.

And you'll kill it!

CHAPTER 9

Committed!

Making a decision (in advance)
to finish the race

CHUCK FARMER WITH JOE BUZZELLO

*"Discipline is doing what you **MUST** do to succeed,*
*regardless of whether you **feel** like it or not."*
—CHUCK FARMER

Several years ago Chuck started entering Spartan races and the Tough Mudder endurance events. He went down this road because he wanted to continue to find ways to challenge himself. Chuck wanted to stay inspired by the work it would take to get ready for the races. He felt that the preparation for each race would help him watch what he was eating and also stay in good physical condition.

His first race was in Atlanta, Georgia. It was a cold, rainy day in March. The very first obstacle he ever encountered was a series of three big holes in the ground that were filled with mud and cold water. He had not prepared for anything like that, but he knew he had to simply put his head down and get to the other side. When he did come out on the other side of the series of ditches, he was caked with mud, partially wet, quite cold...

...and he was hooked!

Chuck LOVES these types of events because they require total commitment, determination, energy and grit, and that's what this chapter is about.

Let's talk about this word...**COMMITMENT**.

But let's look at it from the perspective of being in the shoes of a person who's observed hundreds (and in Joe's case), thousands of commission salespeople, solopreneurs and brick and mortar entrepreneurs.

First, what does the word, "commitment," conjure up in your head? For Chuck, commitment is measured by, "**discipline**."

The level of **dedication** a person brings to the table also defines commitment. It's about being dedicated to do **whatever it takes** to succeed. This extreme mindset of commitment transcends professional endeavors and also transfers over to your personal life—anything that you want to achieve personally. The big paradigm here is that winning salespeople and entrepreneurs FIRST **determine** that they want to do (or achieve) a certain thing, and then they make a series of **definite decisions** to get that thing done. They determine exactly what effort it's going to take to get the job done, what they'll have to put aside and what short-term pain they'll have to endure. The takeaway here is about the **mindset** of **true commitment** in a series of decisions a winner makes up front, before he or she ever gets started.

> *"The big paradigm here is that winning salespeople and entrepreneurs FIRST determine that they want to do (or achieve) a certain thing, and then they make a series of definite decisions to get that thing done."*

It's not a "chicken or the egg" thing for a winner.

Salespeople and entrepreneurs that create massive success in sales don't vacillate on this point. They don't sit around wondering, "What do I do first...do I start the work and then decide if I want to continue—if things are going well? Or do I make the cold hard commitment and decision up front, and then go to work?"

In his role as an organizational sales leader, Chuck does a ton of interviews—searching for that certain type of sales mentality that he can hire to. For Joe and Chuck, many of the other factors don't have much weight. To them, it really doesn't matter what gender a person is, how old they are and what their level of education is.

Great leaders are looking for something else.

In fact, Chuck even goes so far as to tell potential recruits exactly what he's looking for. He tells them, in no uncertain terms, that he wants to attract and hire a person who's looked at the business of commission sales carefully and then made a definite **decision** that this IS what they want to do. Chuck tells them that he's looking to identify a **strong WHY** and a "whatever it takes" attitude.

> ### *Another way of saying this is that we look for a commitment of both mind and heart.*

This is the type of commitment that is very handy a few weeks or months into the journey—that time when things become tough—when the pain of the long race sets in. When a person is faced with a wall or some muddy obstacles, they have a choice. They can either hit the ejector button and QUIT, or they can quickly revisit their WHY—their commitment of mind and heart and then redeploy their energy on the work that gets them to the other side of the mud.

THE KEY CHARACTERISTICS OF COMMITMENT

Let's take a look at a few of the characteristics relevant to commitment and determination. This is about what we've observed and noted about the kind of people that stick and stay in sales—and create wealth.

NOTE: There are no secrets here. This is pretty straightforward stuff!

Extreme DISCIPLINE

For both of us, the trait of **discipline** rises to the top immediately. Chuck likes to use the word, "GRIT." Chuck has a very cool definition of Discipline and grit:

> "Discipline is doing what you MUST do to succeed, regardless of whether you FEEL like it or not."

In commission sales, one of the incredible business advantages that we have is that we can totally **control our schedule**. And that is huge! However, that rare freedom is also **a two edged sword**. When you stop to consider that nobody is going to tell us what time to wake up, get to the office, hit the phones, go out into the field, etc., you MUST have the internal accountability measures and **DISCIPLINE** to be able to **MANAGE** this type of uncommon professional freedom. *(There is an interesting factor to consider here… and it's that this **type of freedom** is one that some people simply can't handle.)*

There are many critical details that one must learn to do their job in sales. You have to learn exactly what to say in order to generate an appointment and you must learn how to engage and discover as you present your products. You will also have to learn how to close—how to ask for the sale and overcome a few objections. There's **a lot to LEARN**!

We believe that all of these things are **TEACHABLE**, but only if someone has the discipline and grit to **show up** every morning, committed to do the work with a smile on their face. Joe and Chuck can't teach that!

As an example, Chuck recently had a great account opportunity that he wanted to involve one of his newer salespeople in. The account was about an hour drive and the appointment was relatively early in the morning. The plan was to have the new salesperson ride with Chuck that morning—to watch and learn. Chuck was going to share some of the commissions earned that morning with the salesperson he invited. The only problem was that the new salesperson **declined his invitation** to join him. Apparently, the meeting was "too early" for the new salesperson!

I know…I know, this is a mind-blowing (extreme) example that we've given you. This seems to be a person that is probably flat out lazy. The person in question is **obviously NOT committed**! But we have learned that there are many (more subtle) degrees of discipline and commitment (or lack thereof) that are less obvious. A person that's going to **make it** in commission sales, must check themselves on the point of extreme discipline every morning they wake up.

OPEN TO ALL OPPORTUNITIES

While discipline rises to the #1 spot, we believe that being **open** to dive in and pursue **all available market opportunities** is a commitment trait that comes in a close second.

To paint the picture of this characteristic, Joe often tells the story of when he entered the insurance industry with Pennsylvania Life in 1979. After he answered a blind ad in the newspaper and passed his state insurance exam, he reported for duty in the Van Nuys office. His second month on the job he was offered the opportunity to travel up to the San Joaquin Valley (Bakersfield) to work on some "customer accounts." Now, when they said, "customer accounts," they actually meant a handful of recently lapsed premium notices. The angle was to send a bright-eyed and bushy tailed dude up to Bakersfield to call on those farmers to get them to renew their coverage...and possibly sell them a few additional riders.

Joe didn't think on the opportunity too long. He figured that (worst case scenario) he could generate a lot of activity fast—talk to a ton of people—get some experience under his belt and maybe cover his gas and motel costs for the week. It turned out to be a great week! He renewed over 80% of the lapsed policies and added new business to almost half of them! He more than covered his gas and the $29-a-night motel room. The production put him at # 6 on the board for all of California that week!

As he made his way back down Highway 5, over the Grapevine and back towards L.A. on that Friday afternoon, he had a huge smile on his face. He later learned that three other agents had turned down the opportunity before they defaulted to him.

We subscribe to the thinking that when you're new and selling opportunities are offered to you, your answer should almost always be, "YES," even before your manager finishes giving you the details. You can become picky later in your career, but upfront, your answer should be YES to almost everything.

Set EMOTIONS Aside – and Revisit the WHY

Let's revisit Chuck's definition of discipline again...

> **"Discipline is doing what you MUST do to succeed, regardless of whether you FEEL like it or not."**

The key word in this definition is "FEEL."

There have probably been times in your life when you have *succumbed* to your feelings versus pushing forward and crossing the finish line. There have been many times that Chuck has experienced this right in the middle of one of his Spartan races. There have been times when he was just physically spent and he simply wanted to **tap out** and quit. He began to ask himself questions like, "Why do I do this to myself?"

These were the times that Chuck went right back to his **WHY**. He revisited the reasons that he decided to participate in those tough endurance races in the first place. So real, hard-core pros have strong WHYs and they conjure up those WHYs when they need to—when emotion and exhaustion creeps in to the equation.

Joe launched a new business model several years back. The business wasn't immediately successful or profitable. In fact, it took Joe a lot longer to find his way to profitability than he anticipated. He's human, so he began to second-guess himself. There was a week or two period of time when Joe felt as if he may not be able to muster up the energy to get the business on solid ground. But then Joe started practicing what he preached. He reflected on some of the reasons he'd started the business. His negative emotions subsided; his energy began to return along with his internal fortitude. He was able to get himself back on track—refocused on the work and determined to cross the finish line.

The rest of the story is that this same business, just two years later, is extremely profitable and growing quickly.

SUMMON ENERGY

Commitment requires **energy**, and that energy comes from **deep inside**.

Chuck likes to say that you can recognize it quickly when a new salesperson has that special energy. He says that it's, "**Layered** right on top of their commitment."

This energy is often displayed in a person's desire to show up and...

- Be *present* at weekly team meetings
- Take part in classroom *training* meetings
- *Pursue* all marketing initiatives
- Go out *in the field* with their manager
- Be extremely *coachable*
- *Stay hungry* to learn *ALL* they can, as *FAST* as they can
- Stay *focused* on the actions that matter

A NO EXCUSES MENTALITY

Salespeople that are truly committed don't wallow in excuses and they certainly don't **WHINE**. Those that are going to WIN in sales don't point fingers externally. They look themselves square in the mirror and look for answers in that same mirror and inside of themselves.

It's one thing for a salesperson to approach their manager and say, "Hey I'm not hitting some of my income or production goals, what can I do differently? What do I need to stop doing?" However, if a salesperson is failing and then (instead of looking inside) all they do is whine, or drown themselves in excuses, they're toast.

Winning salespeople don't barter in excuses. They look for real answers and solutions as they work through their issues.

So, in our humble opinion, here's where the rubber meets the road regarding commitment...

Over the span of our entire careers, we can't even think of **ONE** person that has become successful and created wealth in commission sales, that wasn't 100% committed to the work **up front**. In other words, we have **NEVER** met a person that has become wealthy in our game **that didn't make a firm decision first**, before they ever called on their first prospect.

And we don't believe that this person exists anywhere!

People that develop wealth in sales and entrepreneurial ventures have a reputation of crossing the finish line—getting the job done—not giving up halfway through the journey. They may not be first all the time...and they're probably not gonna' be last...and they are probably going to be cut up and bruised, but they are going to finish what they started.

"People that develop wealth in sales have a reputation of crossing the finish line—getting the job done— not giving up halfway through the journey."

True commitment is about...

- You determining **what** you wish to accomplish *(And WHY)*
- You recognizing the **work** it will take *(And the pain that will come with it)*
- You making the **decision** to do that work *(Up front)*

Nobody can do these things for you and you can't make these decisions halfway through your journey. They must be made **up front** and if you're going to develop wealth in sales, your solemn commitment must be made **in advance** and be one of total **mind** and **heart** to **finish the race** even before it starts.

Section 3

Risk, Change, Urgency + Objectives

Putting yourself **OUT** *there, getting* **UNSTUCK***, developing an* **attitude** *of urgency and developing truly* **meaningful** *goals.*

CHAPTER 10

Risky Business

The mindsets we attach to RISK

JOE BUZZELLO

"Fortune favors the bold."

—LATIN PROVERB

Webster's dictionary defines "risk" as:
...a situation involving exposure to danger

Are there exposures and **risks** involved in the game of commission sales or any entrepreneurial venture?

Yeah. Sure.

You may get a paycheck this week, and then again, you may not.

Are you subjecting yourself to a measure of danger?

Maybe.

If you have a horrible product (or company) behind you, or if you're totally not coachable, or if you sit on your butt, not doing the requisite level of activity, then yeah...there's probably a ton of danger looming. If these factors are in play and you take no action to fix things, then it can be dangerous as heck to your bank balance, credit rating and possibly your marriage. LOL!

So here's how I look at it.

If you purchased this book (and you're actually reading it) then you're probably NOT the kind of person that would *stink it up* that badly. So, bottom line, I'm not sure there's a lot of danger (per se) in commission sales, but there are definite risks to be aware of.

More importantly, we have FLAWED beliefs attached to risk, and that's what this chapter is about. We're going to expose the **flawed thinking** that usually accompanies the concept of risk as it applies to commission-based ventures. In addition to that, we are going to encourage you to form some solid and practical attitudes and philosophies that reduce those risks to quite a manageable level.

OUR OVERALL PERSPECTIVE OF RISK

We have a natural tendency to categorize taking risk as a **negative** thing. When we were younger, some of us were even told that it is "unwise to be a risk taker." While it is a cold, hard fact some risks do NOT pay off, it is critical to remember that many do. So, to come from a place that, "all risk is negative," is not logical and it can **block us** from ever doing anything great in our careers. We will ask you to re-frame risk and place it in the **opportunity** category. We'd like you to believe that measured risk can very well be your path to success.

Reflect back...

Here's an exercise to help you re-frame risk. Grab a yellow pad and find some quiet space. Look back on your life and your career endeavors.
Ask these three questions:

- *Where do I wish I'd been a little **braver**?*

- *Is there a time that I should have **trusted** myself more?*
- *At times, should I have been **less cautious** in the chances I took?*

What comes to mind?

I certainly took some risk to get where I am at today—and where I'm at doesn't suck at all—but even with all of my success I can honestly look back and lament about times I should have taken more risk, **settled less** and **spoke my mind** more often. While having become a self-made multi, multi millionaire is something I'm fiercely proud of, I can still look back and tell you **where and when** I should have been **more courageous.** I've never mentioned this (in writing before) but one move in particular—if I'd had the guts to make it—could have dramatically changed my career (and net worth) for the better. I knew what I should have done...I just didn't do it.

Maybe this resonates with some of you. Hindsight is always 20-20, right?

There are many times we know (in our gut) exactly what it is that we should do, but we **don't** pull the trigger.

Why is this?

When you're already making a lot of money, the status quo can seem easier, softer, less scary...a better option. We are inherently risk opposed. We don't like to expose ourselves—become vulnerable to the unknown. Advanced brain imaging now confirms that we **humans are wired to be risk averse**, so we deem it simpler to keep our mouths shut, our heads down and not take a chance.

We will challenge you to be cognizant of how we are all wired and to look for the opportunities and windows to be more courageous because taking some risk may represent a great opportunity.

Let's take a few minutes to examine five of the most common flawed **perceptions** (and obstacles) regarding the risks in commission sales. We will also suggest how you can mitigate them:

FLAWED perceptions of RISK

1. Potential LOSS looms larger *(in our head)* than any possible GAIN

Our imagination tends to get the better of us on this one. What we focus on most tends to magnify, and what we wind up focusing on most is what can go wrong. We over-estimate the chances of stuff going wrong. Then we begin to think about what we might lose or have to sacrifice. What we fail to assess is that the risk of something **not working out** is often not nearly as high as we estimate—and the odds of it working out well, are often far better.

In addition, we have the nasty habit of **embellishing the consequences** of what might happen if things did go wrong. We arrive at dire, dramatic, worst-case scenarios. Rather than trusting that we have the good judgment to swiftly make corrections if things get off track, our imagination conjures up images of things spiraling out of control while we submissively watch our life burn down. LOL!

We **miscalculate the costs associated with risk and change.** The result is that we often avoid taking on new challenges or pursuing new opportunities. Again, catch yourself and know that we are neurologically wired to overstate how bad things can get.

2. We negate *(or deny)* the cost of a LOST OPPORTUNITY

This is one of those, "It's not so bad," things. In my experience, if things suck for us now and there are a lot of issues in play; they don't tend to get better, **especially if those issues aren't addressed.** This is true in life as well as in business. We deceive ourselves—grab onto the hope that (magically) our circumstances will improve without us taking some action or risk. We're so clever that we cook up wild justifications for why sticking with the **status quo** is a reasonable option. We justify why not putting ourselves at risk of failing (or looking foolish) is a practical way to go.

The problem here is obvious. If we choose to NOT examine where we **could go** if we were willing to take a small risk (or make change), we aren't weighing both sides of the equation. There is often a significant cost when we DON'T pursue an opportunity. For us to ignore the lost opportunity cost or reason it away is simply foolish.

3. *We think SUCCESS will occur without ANY RISK being taken*

Okay, I think you may know this, but I'm going to say it anyway. You may survive in sales, you may even thrive at a low level, but you will NEVER do anything great or build anything of worth without putting yourself out there—without taking some risk. If you think great success is going to just fall into your lap as you wait safely and comfortably for it, you are sadly mistaken—and your helicopter parents lied to you! LOL!

> *"...You will NEVER do anything great or build anything of worth without putting yourself out there—without taking some risk."*

It just doesn't happen that way. You have to go take what you want and that requires courage and a certain amount of risk taking. That's all I'm going to say about this subject.

I lied...here's one more thought on this, you don't achieve all of your dreams by playing it safe!

4. We sometimes equate a FAILED risk to a DEAD END *(no benefit)*

I often have conversations with salespeople or solopreneurs after they took a risk and it didn't exactly pan out. There is a definite divergence in thinking that is quite obvious. One attitude that's taken sounds like...

> *"Well that sucked. I was stupid for trying that. That decision really set me back. I wasted time and money on that one."*

No kidding...I hear this kind of stuff a lot. There's another mindset that sounds very different:

> *"I took a chance and it didn't go that well. But I learned an awful lot from the initiative that can benefit me. I may be able to tweak a few things and reset."*

Here's the thing, we can learn an awful lot from taking risks and putting ourselves out there. However, you have to make an intentional choice
to look for the lessons. And those lessons can be extremely valuable because they can lead you to important, new paths and directions. In addition to the **external opportunities** and recognition taking risk can bring,
it also provides an opportunity for internal growth. I've always felt good
when I've taken risk. You grow each time you step out in faith.

5. We assume taking risk is always a HAPHAZARD practice

This goes back to some of our long-held beliefs. We equate taking risk
to something that feels messy—like a random hit-or-miss type of thing.
We suggest that it SHOULD feel like something very different than that.
First, taking risk should never occur in a vacuum. If you're impetuously
throwing a bunch of ideas out there without stepping back to see the full
picture, shame on you. You must **assess the whole process** or project and
also determine what the end game should look like.

There isn't a lot of benefit from taking risk without **ample preparation**. You have to do your homework and understand the importance of
implementation and follow through. You should also educate yourself on
the possible fall-out.

You may be brand new, or you could be a veteran salesperson who's
continuing to sharpen your sword. (Good for you!) But regardless of their
maturity in the game of sales, there are many (supposedly) bright people
that find themselves **trapped** in a limited bubble of their potential. They
are dissatisfied with where they are at in their career. They may also be
stuck in bad relationships, living lives of quiet desperation. They will tell
you that they didn't choose to be where they are at, however, because of
their choices and actions, that's where they are at.

For anyone that feels a bit trapped or stuck, I'd challenge them to ask
themselves a few more questions:

- *What would I do if I were acting in a **more courageous** manner?*
- *If I **do nothing**, what will my inaction **cost me** a year from now?*

- ***Where*** *is my fear of failure causing me to over-estimate the **size** of risk?*
- *What **calculated risk** would **serve** my business or me now?*

When answers come to mind, take note that they are leading you to a better, more exciting future. You can only move to that NEXT place in your career when you become bolder, more decisive and more courageous.

Will you need to take risks?

YES!

But please keep in mind that we are wired to overestimate the size of the risk and to also underestimate our ability to handle the results. Many years before the life of Jesus Christ, the Chinese philosopher, Lao Tsu wrote:

"You are capable of more than you think."

I want you to **fear** any regrets that you think you may have in your career far more than taking a small risk and failing. In my sales and leadership career of over four decades, I've noted that we always fail far more from faint-heartedness than we do from being bold.

Fortune favors the bold.

Be **BOLD!**

CHAPTER 11

Career Reinvention

Getting unstuck and moving on

DENNIS HARTIN WITH JOE BUZZELLO

*"Just as established products and brands need updating to stay alive and **vibrant**, you periodically need to **refresh** or reinvent yourself."*

—MIREILLE GUILIANO

It can happen to any of us.

After twenty, ten, even as few as five years of doing the **same** thing, selling the same product—for the same company, you can become **STUCK**. You can even begin to think that you are **trapped**. We believe these scenarios are similar to the Stockholm Syndrome—falling in love with your captor. LOL. We become cemented in one place—afraid to make a professional pivot or change.

This can often occur after we've experienced a significant level of success, built solid relationships and created significant loyalties to our leadership. We were rewarded well for working hard, and for many years, our job and the system made sense. We had great confidence in our mother ship and we'd often follow them with blind faith.

Enjoying the Camelot that we thought existed.

Then a funny thing happens.

Our industry, market or company changes.

It happens *slowly*, then much faster near the end. We aren't completely willing to acknowledge all the signs. We're comfortable in our "safe" place. We become risk averse, trapped in what we convince ourselves is a safe and warm cocoon. It becomes harder and harder to fake enthusiasm for the future of our business. We've seen our share of wins and losses, but as we reach a certain age, we begin to question, "Are there any more wins ahead?" "Did we take the right path?" We start to question what our legacy may look like—or if there's even going be any sort of legacy. We hope there may still be enough time. After all, we have confidence and an open mind, but we know that if we're going to make a shift, we've got to take some *risk*.

But there is imperceptible *resistance* at work.

Sometimes this resistance can come from a sense of love and loyalty for the people around us. It can also be about the temporary pain of leaving everything we've ever known and starting over again.

The place we're at (in some ways) is still so damn comfortable.

But the clock is ticking.

> ## *"We're comfortable in our 'safe' place. We become risk averse, trapped in what we convince ourselves is a safe and warm cocoon."*

This condition of getting stuck (or feeling trapped) can happen to any of us, and if you stay in the sales game long enough it surely WILL happen.

Where does this leave us?

How do we step out of the *stagnant* place we may be in and move back into a growth mode? Let's take a moment to outline a few *mindsets* and *attitudes* that hard-core entrepreneurs use to get un-stuck and to reinvent their career direction.

Stop Complaining:

The first thing we'd like you to do (when career reinvention is in order) is to **stop being grouchy**. The energy spent complaining is 100% wasted energy. It's moronic to criticize anything if you don't plan to take **massive action**. Don't do that.

Practice Extreme Recognition: (Get real)

One of the methods we use to shake off the cobwebs is the practice of recognizing the **real and present issues** around us. We have found that this practice (when done right) can be eye-opening and quite cathartic. When considering taking the risk to make a pivot or change, take a good look at (and analyze) the following elements:

- Your **industry** (where it's likely headed)
- Your **company** (as a business vehicle only...nothing more)
- The **products** you're selling (their attractiveness)
- **Your position** in the **evolution** of your skillsets and mindsets
- How your **personal/family commitments** play a role

We'd like you to do this **deep dive of recognition** with little or no emotion involved. Stop drinking the Kool-Aid for a moment and unemotionally work through the process of analysis using the factors/questions listed above.

Create A Transition Plan/Strategy:

We are big on putting key things down **on paper**. When you list out the benefits and risks associated with the pivot or move you're intending to make, two things can happen:

- The **validity** of thinking behind your pivot becomes **clear**
- Your plan acts as a **stimulus** to encourage the change

Consult Your L.B.O.D. (Your Life's Board of Directors)

Before you jump to another industry, company, product line, etc., put your transition plan in front of the 2 – 4 people that serve on your Life's Board of Directors. Get some input and feedback on your future direction from the people that know you well, parents, long time mentors, etc. Both of us have used this invaluable resource more than once. And, oh... ask them to be brutally honest.

A warning: Be careful *who* you share your new vision and direction with and when. Wanting to be honest and open with people is fine, however, not everyone is going to be happy and supportive of your new gig or your changes. Some may even try to *disrupt* your plans.

Pull The Trigger: (Get started, starting over)

When Dennis and Joe have made significant change in their careers there always came a time for them to *jump*. Dennis tells about his good friend, Travis, asking him...

"If you've always known that you should make a move like this, and that you'd be good at it, then what are you waiting for...if not now, when?"

By the way, Dennis didn't have a good answer to that question. Dennis reasoned that he'd been in one place for almost twenty-five years. He'd played it all out. He realized that he had no regrets. That reckoning gave him just enough reason to make the move to what was next for him.

Monitor Your Self-Talk: (The voices in your head)

Sure as heck, if you take some risk and make some bold moves, the voices in your head will kick in. Trust us on this! Some crazy stuff will make its way into your mental coconut. You'll start to think about there being too much competition, you'll ask, "Should I do this now?" The word, "failure" will surely pop into your head. You'll even question if you're, "smart enough or talented enough to pull it all off." A zillion other negative thoughts will buzz around in your brain—all of these thoughts are forms of resistance and they will conspire to stop you from executing on your new direction. First, be 100% aware of this strange phenomenon of resistance in the form of negative thoughts. Then, wipe your head clean and go right back to your plan.

Don't Loiter or Gossip: (Maintain relationships without drama)

Cutting professional ties with old teammates isn't easy, but it has to be done. When you walk away from an organization or division, also resolve to leave the **useless chitchat** behind. You want to give anyone taking your place a fighting chance to succeed without interference—you don't want your successor's future impacted by your words or actions. If they win or lose, it should be due to their initiatives and actions. So this kind of thing—wallowing in the muck and mire of your past gig—is wasted energy. It doesn't help them, it doesn't help you...it's just dumb.

One other thought: As you maintain past relationships, be mindful not to allow the opinions of others impact you in any negative way. Not everyone will be a champion of the moves you're making. Make note that relationship dynamics may change over time, even with some of your preferred relationships.

Disclaimer: *We aren't saying that you have to dissolve personal relationships; we're simply suggesting that you not sink to the depths of the silly rumor mill or the chain of gossip and criticism.*

Create A NEW Set of Peer Mentors:

When you make a major change of industry or organization, you will instantly find yourself on a new **lonely island**. Some of your prior mentors may not be anywhere to be found. It won't be intentional...it just happens. You will feel **isolated** for a short time. Our strong advice to you would be for you to begin to immediately reach out to the best and brightest in your new circle of influence. Create a new group of **peer Sherpa guides** as quickly as you can.

Remember...**you have incredible gifts** to offer to others and vice versa. Get out there and find the people that you need to be around and share meaningful ideas with. Genuine relationships matter more than ever today, but we oftentimes get caught up in collecting numerous superficial connections. We should strive for connection with *real people* you can trust, and we should strive to be that kind of person and friend to others.

> *"Genuine relationships matter more than ever today, but we oftentimes get caught up in collecting numerous superficial connections."*

Develop NEW Paradigms:

After you make the kind of career pivot or reinvention we are talking about, it's easy to bring **OLD** ideas with you. You can spend a great deal of time on business models that don't work or matter. A major amount of your time and energy can easily be spent reflecting back on the "old days" and the old paradigms that won't apply, work or be helpful. Bottom line, pulling your old world (or people) into your new world typically doesn't work and it usually proves to be a gigantic waste of time.

To truly **reinvent** yourself (and your career) you have to be willing to take the risk of starting over from the ground up. You'll have to block out some of what you *think* you know and begin to see everything through a new lens—perspective. You may be starting over and your old title and leverage may be useless in your new world. It sounds bleak—starting over at the bottom—but it's not. When you have nowhere to go but *up*, and you accept that, and you begin seeking out NEW ways of thinking, it's pretty liberating!

> *"Bottom line, pulling your old world (or people) into your new world typically doesn't work and it usually proves to be a gigantic waste of time."*

Do The Work: (Put in your 10,000 hours)

Lastly, we want to remind you that simply accepting that you're stuck and that you need to take some risk and make a change doesn't necessarily get you *where* you want to go.

But, doing a massive amount of work ***does***.

So we'd like to remind you that you will need to put 10,000 hours into your new gig, just like you did in your prior gig.

We have studied this subject of **career reinvention** and the risks that we must take to move forward. We have concluded that immersing yourself in more educational opportunities and making vital connections is key after you make the jump. Be a sponge and invest heavily in your professional and personal development. We feel that it is essential to become an *expert* in your new world as quickly as you can.

What we would also caution you on is spending too much time getting ready to get ready. LOL! Recognize that this kind of thing is **procrastination** and procrastination is a **coping mechanism** for your fear and insecurity about your ability to execute. You will resist making the needed changes in your career and begin to **rationalize** your stagnancy with stuff that sounds good on the surface.

But it's all BS. LOL!

You must realize that you probably know ***way more*** than needed to make the jump and make it work. We learn more by doing than hearing anyway. Career reinvention becomes necessary for all of us at some juncture. Taking some calculated risk and getting unstuck is our path forward and we all know that our biggest risk is not taking any risk at all.

But that kinda' sucks...

...and it's no fun.

CHAPTER 12

An Attitude of Urgency

The remedy for procrastination

KATIE ANDERSON WITH JOE BUZZELLO

*"Without a sense of urgency, desire **loses** its value."*

—JIM ROHN

Procrastination is a common coping mechanism—it's easy, comfortable—it seems okay...then it turns into a nasty **disease**, and then that disease kills your sales career.

We know...this concept may be new to you.

You've probably never had anyone float this premise by you in this **direct** and unfiltered a manner. However, we believe this principle is critical to understand and we want to hit you right between the eyes with it. We believe that if a salesperson ignores the importance of developing **an attitude of urgency**, they'll probably spend their time

85

earning a degree in procrastination from "Not Yet University" and then set up camp in "Laterville, USA" where they'll suffer through a career loaded with mediocrity...and mediocrity is probably their best-case scenario.

There are many ways in which salespeople **ENTER** the world of commission sales. In some cases, they *fall into* it by happenstance—they weren't considering sales—but the interviewer was awesome and the job sounded interesting. In other cases there was a natural pull to sales—the person was told that he or she had a, "knack for sales," or told something equally pedestrian. Some were actually targeted and recruited by a sales leader—one who then painted a utopian picture of the wonder that would result if they committed to a life in sales.

Regardless of how you *entered* the world of commission sales (or what your mindsets and attitudes were upon your glorious entrance), the bottom line is, if you don't develop a sense of urgency about things, your sales career will **end** before it ever begins.

This chapter will concentrate on the model of attaching URGENCY (as a strong ATTITUDE) to the actions that *drive* your business forward. The most successful sales professionals that we have had the pleasure of hiring and mentoring would all agree that sales is a game that requires:

- Commitment
- Tenacity
- Discipline
- Skillsets

And sure...we can probably add ten other attributes to this list, but like most things that look good on paper, these elements can still result in a *crash and burn* failure if one **attitudinal element** doesn't strongly exist in the background. If a **sense of urgency** isn't being fostered, maintained and practiced on a daily basis, then the coping mechanism of procrastination will begin to *creep in* and eventually become your default mindset. Then you're toast!

"If a sense of urgency isn't being maintained and practiced on a daily basis, then the coping mechanism of procrastination will begin to creep in and eventually become your default mindset. Then you're toast!"

So let's jump into this **"sense of urgency"** thing (as an attitude) and take a quick look at some of the behavioral psychology behind it—what it can **look**, **sound** and **feel** like. For this example, we'll feature two very recognizable but fictitious characters named, **"Procrastinating Patty,"** and, **"Timely Tim."** As we move through the patterns of these two personas, we'd like you to take notice of the differences that a sense of urgency can make for each of them.

By the way, we will mention that from the outside (during any given measured sales period), these two characters can appear to be very **similar**. They both seem successful and committed to their professions. They can each post some level of decent sales results for their organizations. They have good sales skills—they can sell anything to anyone as long as they believe in their company and what they're selling.

The **differences**, however, become more noticeable when you take a look under the hood. The disparities lie within their handling of key sales processes such as:

- *Daily **calendar disciplines***
- *Levels of **sustained** key **activities***
- *Management of **sales cycles***
- *Advanced **pipeline** practices*

These variances are indicative of the **presence** of (or **lack** thereof) a **sense of urgency**, or what we like to call, an ATTITUDE of urgency—and where that urgency is directed.

So let's take a look at these two characters:

"Procrastinating Patty"

Patty works hard enough, however she's a procrastinator. One of the bad habits she fell into early in her sales career was that of assigning **priority** to certain tasks that ultimately wouldn't move the needle for her business. She would "major in the minors." This is Joe's old saying for people that spend a **major** amount of time on things of **minor** importance. Patty adopted the habit of poor prioritization—giving importance to items we may call, "fires" or "shiny objects."

So these "minor" things would occupy her time. (And her mind) They would give her a false sense of execution—and she'd assign no urgency to the fundamental actions and activities that would otherwise move her business **forward**.

The obvious driver for any new (or evolving) salesperson is **prospecting**—filling the pipeline. For Patty, there was no sense of urgency allotted to this key task. (It happened when it happened) She would prospect a great deal **MORE** when her sales results were **down** and prospect a great deal **LESS** when her sales were **up**. She would say things like...

"I need to take care of this (minor thing) now. I'll get around to prospecting when I'm done with this."

As a result of Patty **not** establishing a **steady** sense of urgency about relentless growth issues—and because she historically only **reacted** when her pipeline (and checking account) were bone-dry, her sales results felt like a wild roller coaster ride. This sounds kind of exhausting, doesn't it?

So if you're following the example we're laying out, there are financial and emotional ramifications for Patty's defective approach to what's important. She isn't properly recognizing what **should** be considered URGENT and which tasks should be categorized as non-essential. (And be performed during **non-prime time**) Patty's business is constantly *pulling her* one direction or another. Because of the fact that she has not attached an attitude of urgency to the true growth drivers of her business, Patty is allowing her business to **RUN** her instead of her being able to effectively run the business she wishes to build.

But let's dig deeper. Let's examine **WHY** Patty's sense of urgency for the right things—the essential business drivers—slowly dissipated into the undesirable habit of procrastination.

Psychologists tell us that when **urgency** isn't placed behind the **right actions** in life and business and they aren't practiced daily, it becomes more naturally supported (and accepted) for a person to delay key decisions, to *absolve* yourself from taking action, or to even *slow* your current activities and calendar. To say this in plainer language, we begin to create our own little comfortable environment of weakness—and then we become a total **PRODUCT** of that environment.

By the way, when we *think* and *do* stuff like this, we are rarely fooling ourselves. Patty will actually wake up to what's really going on at some point. However, she's made a short-term decision to **COPE** with things she doesn't feel comfortable doing, utilizing that handy tool of procrastination. So her attitudinal habit is fully baked in the oven for her along with all of the tangent bad habits that accompany it.

Look, we get it...it's definitely a part of our human nature to put off the "hard" tasks till mañana. At first, we get away with it. In fact, we've seen salespeople do "okay" for years without a sense of urgency, however, this practice will eventually kill Patty's long-term path to real wealth and freedom. A great career—one where you develop significant prosperity—isn't sustainable in commission-based sales unless you develop the proper attitude of urgency.

And Patty hasn't developed it.

"Timely Tim"

On the other hand, there is this dude named, *Timely Tim*. He is also a hard worker, but unlike Patty, he rarely procrastinates. This poor habit (and coping mechanism) never became part of his mental make up—it never occurred to him to procrastinate on essential tasks. From day one in sales his trainer, "Katie," mentored him regarding which **activities** were critical to his success initially and also on a long-term basis. As a result, he has always identified and prioritized what mattered, and those pesky, "fires" that preoccupy Patty never distracted him from relentlessly pursuing the actions that drove his business forward.

Tim lives in a highly **organized** world, one that includes lists, reminders, data and prioritization. He applies a sense of urgency to everything that he knows is essential to his long-term growth. When he began his sales career, Katie challenged him to make a definite choice to *value* his prospecting activities and initiatives as a **TOP priority**, even when his sales were **up**.

As a result of this advice, he quickly developed a strong sense of urgency about the **daily task** of filling the pipeline and keeping it full. He became relentless about these types of identifiable business drivers. For Tim, prospecting and other key drivers don't just *"happen when they happen,"* or when he feels that he can, "get around to it." Tim's head works very differently than Patty's. He has established flawless mindsets regarding prospecting and other essential growth drivers. Tim is often overheard saying things such as:

> *"I identify what absolutely needs to happen inside of my business to keep it moving forward. I make those things URGENT and a priority. Everything else revolves around those things...those things can't wait."*

Unlike Patty, Tim is not in the habit of *fooling* himself. Tim has a firm handle on the attitude of URGENCY. When he awakes each morning, he is in a **hurry** to build his business by focusing on the right (essential) drivers. Tim has made a solid long-term decision to focus on what moves the needle inside of his business and as such, he doesn't need a **coping mechanism** such as **procrastination**. Tim doesn't default to only doing the things that are comfortable for him. He doesn't put off the "hard" tasks. He is aware that this type of mentality is a long walk on a short pier. He knows that this type of weakness would kill his momentum and possibly kill his career.

Tim wants to develop great wealth and financial independence in his career and he knows this will only happen if he can stay in the game long-term. He also knows that to stay in the game long-term you must develop flawless attitudes and habits that allow for the business to have year-over-year compound growth. Tim knows that you have to create an effective and proper **attitude of urgency** to make all of this happen. Tim completely understands that long-term growth and permanent wealth doesn't "just happen" if you aren't relentlessly and urgently growing your business.

Let's encapsulate the paths of these two wonderful (and not so fictional) characters, Patty and Tim. They both work HARD, right? They both have reasonably decent competencies and skillsets and they are both committed to their profession. However, if we take a giant step backward, and production numbers don't blind us, it's apparent that **their paths will eventually separate**.

Somebody like Tim is building a business based on fined-tuned mindsets, attitudes and behaviors. On the other hand, Patty's career has been that of **selling things**—chasing the wild swings in production. She simply hasn't developed a business (and a way of thinking and acting) the way higher-level entrepreneurs do. Any situational success for Patty can be credited to her great personality, solid selling skills and perhaps a little luck here and there. It will be difficult for Patty to kick the procrastination habit and survive (and scale) long-term if she doesn't first adopt a strong sense of urgency and attach it to the things that are essential.

Let's take a look at **three key methods** that you can employ to begin to adopt and apply an **attitude of urgency** and utilize this mindset to remedy the disease of procrastination:

Identify the DRIVERS:

If we first identify what really *drives* our business forward, then we have 80% of the battle won! Typically, if you are NEW in sales (first few years) this is almost always going to revolve around prospecting and securing time and attention with qualified decision makers. However, you get to work with your coach or mentor and decide what your drivers are.

Establish YOUR attitude on URGENCY:

Can you sit down, create some quiet space, and **draft a brief statement** of what urgency means to you inside of your business right now? What are your pillars of urgency? What actions are you willing to prioritize inside of your business (daily and weekly) to move it forward? With your STRONG (written) attitude, how will you ensure that you don't default into a state of procrastination?

Write down your version of an **attitude of urgency**. Then keep it where you can see it everyday!

Be cognizant of what feels COMFORTABLE:

Recognize that there may be times that you begin to slip into a place of mental **relaxation**. What we mean is that you may (at some point) backslide into putting essential things **off**. You may even start to rationalize or justify these actions. This may typically happen when you are physically or mentally **tired** or if you haphazardly fall into a mild slump.

So catch yourself! Take notice if you start to "put off" some of the more **uncomfortable** tasks for more **comfortable** ones. Become completely cognizant of the fact that when you're doing a lot of "comfortable" stuff you are rarely doing the things that will help your business **GROW** or **scale**.

If we determine that "urgency" is synonymous with importance, seriousness, persistence and all of the other cool growth elements, then it's also logical that urgency is a **VITAL** piece of our sales attitudes and mindsets. Further, if we choose NOT to *apply* a sense of urgency to our business we are, by default, making a choice to operate in the opposite fashion, focusing on things that may be unimportant, insignificant, unproductive or trivial.

If we still haven't sold you **yet** on the importance of developing an attitude of urgency, then consider these points:

- Without a sense of urgency we let the **ebb and flow** of our business control us.

- Without a sense of urgency we have **no reason** to push ourselves—continue to knock on those last ten doors of the day, or *dial for dollars* on those last twenty phone numbers.
- Without a sense of urgency we **slow** down—we lose momentum.

And lastly, as Jim Rohn has told us, "Without a sense of urgency, **desire** loses its value."

What this really means is that you can **WISH** in one bucket, and consistently load the **right kind of work** into the other bucket and only one of those buckets will fill up and stay full. The beautiful thing about creating and adopting a sense of urgency about your work is that the coping mechanism of procrastination melts away—it can't co-exist.

Your attitude of urgency is a complete and total antidote for it!

"The beautiful thing about creating and adopting a sense of urgency about your work is that the coping mechanism of procrastination melts away—it can't co-exist."

We have seen many hopeful people enter the game of commission sales. Those that really succeed tend to be in a *hurry* to get started—they can't wait to get to work—get their hands dirty. We've also noted that once they start to LIVE inside of this attitude that we call a "sense of urgency" they also tend to **stay hungry** and grow like crazy.

Joe and Katie have been in direct sales for over (a combined) sixty years. They're still acting on the mindset of urgency today—they can't wait to do the uncomfortable stuff—to hit the important work head-on! They don't put essential things off.

How about you?

Are you committed to build your business with an "attitude of urgency"?

CHAPTER 13

A Few Meaningful Objectives

*Focusing on what's
important to YOU*

EMILY EVANS WITH JOE BUZZELLO

*"If you tune into your purpose and actually **align** with
it, setting goals so that your vision is an expression of
that purpose, then life flows much more easily."*

—JACK CANFIELD

In professional sales and small business ventures, we have observed several interesting goal-setting mindsets and phenomena. What we've seen generally falls into three categories:

Rudderless

We call the first category, "Rudderless," because in this scenario, there is ZERO goal setting being done. The person in this example is *rudderless*. There is no mentor or hierarchy involved to help them establish meaningful goals. There are no checkpoints, markers or milestones during year one and beyond. (If they make it past year one!)

Force-Fed

Another category exists that we will refer to as "Force-Fed goals." In this second grouping a person is **TOLD** what objectives he or she should establish and pursue. There is typically little or no input asked for.

Heaped

At the far end of the spectrum we see people that have typically (either through their own doing and/or other people's input) created far TOO MANY goals. In addition to the objectives being too numerous, they're often too fuzzy and/or difficult to track. Most importantly, they're not meaningful or pertinent to the person's survival or happiness. They are simply "heaped" on the back of a person, crushing them.

Obviously, we don't feel that any of the aforementioned objective seeking, goal-setting categories are beneficial for your survival and ultimate success. While it's quite apparent that being rudderless is not a great place to be (and may lead to your extinction) we also don't like having TOO MANY goals. We think this also kind of sucks. However, the worst type is definitely the Force-Fed category. This is because you have NO ownership of what you are working towards.

This mindset is about determining what's important to you and focusing on the benchmarks that will get you there. Unless you completely understand the game you're in, and then take a moment to look inside of yourself, you cannot possibly establish the few meaningful objectives that will enable you to finish the race.

> *"Unless you completely understand the game you're in, and then take a moment to look inside of yourself, you cannot possibly establish the few meaningful objectives that will enable you to finish the race."*

And that's the primary message of this chapter.

We'd like you to establish the right kind of goal-seeking mindset and attitude. We want you to establish a few clear and reasonable objectives that are also aligned with your **core purpose** for building your business—ones that YOU truly have **ownership** of.

We *love* strategic planning and setting goals and we're good at it. It makes our brains happy. However, we do understand that not everyone feels the same way, nor have they evolved the methods to do it properly. A friend of Emily's recently posted a question that she thought was interesting, cute and funny. Her friend asked, "I'm sitting down to do some goal planning...uh, how do I even start?" LOL! Most newer salespeople struggle with planning, projecting and goal setting. Emily's answer to her friend was quite straightforward and contained a great deal of wisdom. She responded...

> *"...Why don't you begin with the END in mind."*

So, if we're counseling a newer salesperson on how to *think* about their **initial** and **future** goals, we may ask them to reflect on the following questions: *(Broken down into the following time periods)*

Year 1: *(Short-term)*

- *How do I want my 1ˢᵗ year to END?*
- *What would **success** look like to me personally?*
- *What key **benchmarks** will ensure my SURVIVAL?*
- *What are the MAJOR objectives (that when accomplished) would have a tremendous IMPACT on my business?*

During year 1, it is all about *surviving* to fight another battle. It's caveman time...how can I bring some food home tonight? Virtually all of your goals and objectives should be focused on survival...and you should have just a few major objectives. *(1 or 2 at most)*

2 – 5 Years: *(Near-term)*

- Where do I **visualize** myself/my business being in 2 – 5 years?
- What do I want to **BUILD**?
  - What will the business **look** like? *(Metrics)*
    - What's my **% growth** goal for next year?
    - What is that gross production #?
    - How much of my goal will be made up by **existing** customers?
    - How many **new clients**/accounts do I need to hit that goal?
  - What **elements** need to be added?
  - Which systems will be needed to make it more **sustainable**?
  - **What people** do I need to add to my business?
- What do I need to **BECOME** in the process?
  - How will I need to grow **professionally**?
  - What **personal** growth will have to take place?
- How will my **lifestyle** begin to change?
- Have I started a self-employed retirement plan? **(SEP)**
- Do we have a **college-funding** plan in place?

When you've figured out how to stick and stay, it then becomes more about what you want to build and become. You begin working **ON** your business versus just **IN** it. Your major objectives should reflect those things.

10 + Years: *(Long-term)*

- At what age do I want to establish **financial freedom**?
  - What is my **NUMBER**?
  - Where am I at **now**?

- How can I **ensure** that we hit our number?
- What **DIRECTION** do I need to take my business?
  - Do I have the **right people** in place?
  - Are my **processes** + **systems** hard wired?
- What is **most important** to me personally now?
  - Where do I want to **travel**?
  - What experiences do I want to have?
  - What **people** do I want to spend the most **time** with?
  - Are my professional goals **aligned** with my personal/family objectives?
- What is my **exit** strategy?

The questions you start to ask and the goals/objectives you begin to establish at the 10 year + mark are different than those at the one or two year mark. Your objectives are far more about making the business an effective **vehicle** for your life, lifestyle and family. We also begin to look at what's NEXT.

As you soak in the questions you'll ask at different intervals in time, you can see how your goal setting can shift. While your objectives will change, we'd like to make sure that three **significant guidelines** remain constant:

- **Make sure your goals are PERSONAL** (You OWN them!)
- **Ensure that they are CLEAR** (Easy to understand)
- **Only FOCUS on 1 or 2 MAJOR objectives at a time**

Joe often reminds people that, "If everything is a priority, then NOTHING is a priority." So if you are new to setting goals or objectives (or you are re-calibrating your business) you may want to practice these three important goal-setting steps:

1. Prioritize

Write any and all of your objectives down on paper, then select the one or two goals that, when accomplished, would have an **overwhelming impact** on your business—ones that would totally move the needle forward.

2.   *Clarify + Create A Deadline*

Make sure your major objective is **clear** enough so almost anyone (inside or outside of your business) could understand it. Make sure it takes you from one point to another. (Points "A" and "B")

Then create a deadline for the major objective. For example, "I want to develop 30 new clients/accounts by the end of this year." The objective is clear and it has an **expiration** date.

3.   *Announce + Visualize*

Tell other (**key**) people about your specific goals. The people that we suggest you share your objectives with are **stakeholders** and **supporters** such as hierarchy, mentors, spouses, close friends, etc. When you talk about your exact objectives with someone else on a regular basis, it makes them **real** and you also become *hung by your tongue*—speaking your intended new world into existence.

After you've announced your goals, then **display** them in **visual format** all around you. These are pictures or word text that depicts what you want. Place reminders and prompts where you'll be sure to see them several times per day. We like the refrigerator, the bathroom mirror and also in a prominent place in your office.

Hopefully, this chapter has supplied you with practical methods that will help you become more effective in short-term, near-term and long-term goal setting. More than that, we're hoping you come away from this short chapter lesson with something even better. We're hoping that you adopt a high-level mindset that can blanket all of your thinking on establishing objectives.

In summary, we'd LOVE it if you adopt the mindset that the few major objectives that you establish MUST be **MEANINGFUL** to you and they should also be **aligned** to your purpose of building the business.

SECTION 4

Coachability, The Work + Accountability

Becoming totally **OPEN** *to mentorship, understanding the VALUE of* **WORK**, *and taking complete* **responsibility** *for your career.*

CHAPTER 14

Becoming Completely Coachable

Moving to the WINNING end of the spectrum

CHRISTIE MARZARI WITH JOE BUZZELLO

*"My best skill was that I was **coachable**. I was a sponge."*

—MICHAEL JORDAN

At a CAP Equation mastermind meeting in Scottsdale, in the summer of 2019, a few of the co-authors of this book pondered the question...

"Is being coachable an ATTITUDE, or is it a COMPETENCY?"

We were striving to place **COACHABILITY** in the proper category inside of The CAP Equation methodology. After a small amount of debate, the group quickly settled on the answer...

...definitely an attitude!

You can argue that most people are cognizant enough (and intelligent enough) to know they need mentorship. After all, what moron would openly profess that they "know it all" and wouldn't benefit from an experienced coach, mentor or trainer? In fact, most new salespeople say all of the right things—they posture that they are "open" and "coachable." But does that really mean they're coachable—just because they say they are? They can meet regularly with their hierarchy, read books, attend seminars and go through the motions, but do those actions actually translate into and guarantee true coachability?

From our perspective **it doesn't**.

We've seen hundreds of salespeople do and say all the right things relevant to coachability, and still fall way short of being the "sponge" that Michael Jordan references above. So being **completely coachable** is not about simply showing up for the donuts and coffee, it's a **total mindset**. There is a figurative **coaching spectrum** that we loosely refer to, and many new salespeople enter the game and **exist** for many years—telling people they're coachable—however, they actually rank quite low on the coachability spectrum.

Your next question may sound like...

"Why would a person enter a risky proposition like commission sales (many with little or no experience), be presented with a great coach willing to help them, and then not be completely open?"

Logical enough question!

We'll break this down the best way we can for you. We believe there are several reasons people may **resist** or **reject** coaching.

It can be Humbling

You guessed it—**ego** comes into play. A person may have been quasi-successful in another business, or perhaps they hold an advanced degree or other academic sheepskins. It may be that they come from money—a silver spoon in their mouth. It can be a matter of their scripting—mommy and daddy always telling them how talented they are. Regardless of the root cause, when ego kicks in, it can prohibit them from being open—they may feel that they're placing themselves in a submissive position.

If you submit yourself to a coach who has achieved something that you **wish** to accomplish, you must "humble" yourself to a small degree. Some people have a challenge with this because they perceive that being humble is a **weakness**. What's ironic is, admitting that you don't know how to do something is one of the **strongest** characteristics you can have when you are new. And what's even more ironic is that, if you DON'T humble yourself to experienced people, you will **remain WEAK** in your skillsets and **eventually fail** to accomplish what you set out to do.

> *"...If you DON'T humble yourself to experienced people, you will remain WEAK in your skillsets and eventually fail to accomplish what you set out to do."*

Change May Take Place

I think you may be aware that many of us are **abhorrent** to change. Many of us have a weird relationship with change. We're comfortable with the **way** things **are**. They're just fine. But this new mentor may ask us to change and that's downright uncomfortable. So we resist—make up excuses of why that **won't** work for us...or we simply don't show up for coaching. The truth is, almost every person that enters the commission sales game is going to have to **change** a myriad of things about their behavior and practices, and we must realize going in, that if we don't adjust (change) some of those behaviors, we run a huge risk of crashing and burning.

The key here is to understand that, just because we've always done things (and thought about things) one certain way, it doesn't mean it's the best, or even the **right** way.

They Don't Really Want Help (They Want Validation)

Very early in our leadership careers we were taught how to identify salespeople who weren't open to coaching. These nice people say that they want direction, but when you begin the process of asking questions to determine if they're at all self-aware—being honest with you—it's not there. They aren't with you to take (and apply) the lessons. In fact, they do most of the talking. They like the sessions—the attention. They will go out in the field with you and go through the motions, but they are looking for something else other than real coaching. They want you to **validate** their thinking—tell them how smart they are. They aren't ready for coaching. They just want to be flattered.

Prior Bad Experience

We must realize that some of the people we lay hands on may have had a poor (or negative) experience with a prior coach or mentor. Their former, so called, "coach" may have been well meaning but inept. They may have been demeaning or condescending. They could have been unethical or downright dishonest. We must take into consideration that a prior bad experience can come into play here.

There may be a few more reasons people aren't coachable, but you get the point. So this is a sort of, *"if the shoe fits, wear it,"* kind of thing. If you currently fall into (or have fallen into) one of these categories, you at least know WHO you are, and you can begin to repair your own thinking.

Joe has a favorite saying: "When the student is ready, the teacher appears." There's a lot packed into that statement for both parties. First, if the student isn't open, it doesn't matter who's in front of them—it can be Tony Robbins or Zig Ziglar and that student would turn a blind eye. The other lesson here is that, if you are a coach or trainer, you'd better determine who's **ready** to be coached, because if you don't, you could waste a great deal of your valuable time.

"When the student is ready, the teacher appears."

So there's a lot going on here, but what's really critical is that you get the coaching and support you need. Hence, we are going to give you a quick checklist of **behavioral mindsets** on the subject of **coachability** that you can consider and adopt.

Take A Small Risk

Why not shake things up in your life? You're making a big change. Why would you shut down to great new ideas? You should look at coaching as something **exciting**, just like a kid on Christmas morning. Become enthusiastic to see the potential **inside of you** that can be unleashed by the right coach.

Seek Out the RIGHT Mentors

Make sure that your coach has some **fruit on their tree**. If you are assigned a coach or trainer that isn't successful, ask them for someone else, or simply go grab a **peer** mentor. Consider hiring an outside coach. If you are **inside** of an organization (an intrepreneur) and they won't give you a proven mentor, then maybe you need to leave. But don't sit there, using BS excuses and fail...and don't settle for a bad coach.

Dig Into the Process

The most important part of this whole enchilada is how you respond to a viable proven coach that's trying to help you. So we'd like you to actually consider your mindsets and behaviors as your coach is dispensing his or her wisdom. Do you listen to intentionally *learn* and *understand* or are you just there? Do you ask additional questions to uncover more information about the area you are being coached in? We are suggesting that you make a mindset decision to be totally **PRESENT** for (and intently engaged in) any and all coaching sessions.

Park Your EGO at the Door!

For the love of God...please, please, please, park your ego at the door. Go into each session without feeling the need to **DEFEND** things. People like that are so annoying to a good coach. Look...you **are** where you **are**. You jumped into commission sales so that you could forge a new path to wealth. But you're going to sit in front of a person who's trying to help you get there and second-guess them—argue with them? Sheesh.

Don't Take Anything Personally

When a competent coach is mentoring you, he or she may say some things you **need** to hear—so that you can survive and eventually thrive. Develop an attitude that enables you to have a **thick skin**.

In many cases, a great coach will challenge you to improve both process and performance. You should be aware that process improvement is usually **easier to swallow**, as it does not get quite so personal. On the other hand, huge growth can come from those things going on inside of you. You need honest feedback from a coach and you'll need to spend some time on self-reflection. Not easy stuff, but you can make it easier by not being so defensive and so hypersensitive.

Apply What You Learn

Finally, you can do all of the right things, but leave one element out. We've seen people take the risk of opening up, find the right mentor, become present, park their ego, only to **fail** to cross the finish line. You WIN with great coaching when you actually **step out on faith** and DO the things that your coach is asking you to do. Regardless of how uncomfortable new thoughts and actions may seem, try them—put them into play.

We're asking you to make a **decision** to apply what you are learning. Put the words, strategies, methods and tactics to work—**take massive action** on the things you and your coach are discovering together. Salespeople that become wealthy **actually do something** with the great information they receive. They don't sit on it—they apply it—and then they give feedback to those who have coached them.

There are quite a few things that can get in the way of you becoming completely coachable, and we want you to be aware of those detrimental behaviors. We want you to **replace them** with **productive mindsets** and attitudes that can change everything for you.

Last thought on this...

The best and the brightest stars in athletics, entertainment and business all have high-level coaches. Even after they reach the zenith of their respective fields, they still retain coaches and visit with them often. **They are totally and completely coachable**. Even if they are #1 in the world at their game, they park their ego at the door and eagerly apply the new tools and mindsets they are discovering about their sport, craft or themselves.

This is the mindset we'd like you to **emulate**.

Become totally and **completely coachable** in every way...

...and wealth will follow!

CHAPTER 15

Showing Up

Understanding the VALUE of the work

LEON DAVIDSON WITH JOE BUZZELLO

*"**Work ethic** is important because, unlike intelligence, athleticism, charisma, or any other natural attribute, it's a **choice**."*

—MIKE ROWE

A sales manager recruits you, and then they begin their job of becoming your trainer, coach, supporter and guru. Their role serves many critical functions. They're the person who'll identify the land mines that you might otherwise trip over and they also pick you up when you fall. They are excited to start the process of helping you become the next "rock star". A good trainer knows exactly what skillsets their newly assigned salesperson needs to learn (and in what order), so that they can master the proficiencies necessary to achieve their goals.

However, having a mentor is only half of the equation. A salesperson MUST **show up**, and they must quickly develop a mindset about the **value of the work** and their willingness to **DO** the work!

> *"A salesperson MUST show up, and they must quickly develop a mindset about the value of the work and their willingness to DO the work!"*

The old saying, "Showing up is half the battle", is certainly true, but we'd like to take this endearing proverb a bit deeper. We'd like you to show up with a baked-in-the-oven mindset about **the work**. We'd like you to **establish a paradigm** on this subject, and that's what we will focus on in this chapter.

We believe that most people make a **choice** to **DO** or **NOT** do the work, and it's not always a completely **conscious** decision. The choice is influenced by many factors. It can be a person's scripting, which essentially means the way you were raised and the voices in your head...usually called "parents".

> *"We believe that most people make a choice to DO or NOT do the work, and it's not always a completely conscious decision."*

We believe that your **environment** plays an equally significant part in all of this. It's about being intentional with regard to the **people** you associate with—let into your world—and the **input** you take in.

We were lucky to be raised by parents that dispensed sage wisdom—stuff like, "You only get out of life what you put into it." Our parents told us that, "If you commit to something, then you give it your all." They would compel us to not, "short-change," the work we decided to do. We were also lucky to have early surroundings that fostered our **beliefs** of what we could do with our lives. So we were fortunate...our **scripting** was awesome. However, they don't make parents like they used to! LOL!

EARLY SCRIPTING

Leon has a professional sports background. His teammates and coaches heavily influenced him. He **watched** the way successful athletes went about their craft. He noticed that the top tier stars didn't just put in minimum required time at scheduled practices. Instead, they showed up early and they stayed late. He began to **emulate** them. He soon began to feel the incredible inner satisfaction that you can only feel when you know you're traveling the **extra mile**—doing more work than the average player.

All of his great work ethic earned Leon a professional baseball tryout. It happened in Long Beach, California during the summer of 1972. Ironically, the team that invited him to the tryout didn't offer him a contract, but another team did! Leon was off to rookie ball—a real professional—getting paid...not much, but getting paid.

During his first year, Leon noticed how those players who worked significantly harder (the tireless ones) moved up faster. Leon realized he needed to stay on the grow and keep learning to be viewed as a viable prospect. He decided he'd learn to throw the knuckleball. By the way, if you're not a baseball aficionado, we have to tell you that this is not an easy pitch to master. Leon went about the work—completely willing to do what it took to get it right. Roughly seventy-five hours of practice time later, he could throw a pretty good knuckleball, which attracted a lot of positive attention from team officials. Unfortunately, due to injuries, Leon's baseball career eventually stalled at the 'single A' level, but he learned valuable life lessons from that experience—some that would benefit him professionally over the years.

Joe also had some amazing work ethic scripting as he grew up. His father was a phenomenal role model for him. He worked hard as an aerospace engineer, rarely missing a day of work and often bringing some of his work home. Joe's mother was the energizer bunny, always doing what it took and then some to create a wonderful home environment. He was scripted to stay in motion and give 110%.

Joe became addicted to golf in his teens, but he was far from a natural golfer. Between the ages of thirteen and eighteen he either played or practiced at least six days a week. He hit as many as 250 balls a day on the range. Because there was no money for expensive golf lessons, Joe was self-taught, watching better golfer's swings, bugging them—asking them questions until they became irritated with him. Joe eventually made the varsity team during his junior year in high school. He became a fairly good golfer and in later years, he served as a Southern California section PGA teaching professional.

TAKING THE ENTREPRENEUR'S + LEADER'S PATH

By 1979, both Joe and Leon had joined the great-unwashed ranks of the entrepreneurial world. Joe got his insurance license and took a commission sales gig—getting hired by the Pennsylvania Life Company. He went through their cold calling boot camp (from hell) and learned how to sell $39 accident policies down the street. Leon began imprinting names and numbers on the backs of uniforms and selling them to sports teams in his community.

They were off and running.

Leon and Joe upgraded themselves from one gig to the next, both of them ultimately finding their way into the employee benefits industry, and eventually each of them became leaders with their companies. In his executive management role, Joe was able to apply so much of what he learned from his scripting, parents, experiences, mentors and peers. He had created a **rock solid mindset** about doing the work. As his father had advised him, Joe never quit anything without creating some kind of 'win' first. He was always able to **extract** some kind of **value** out of every situation and walk away with his head held high.

Bottom line, Joe never failed at anything because he wasn't willing to do the work.

> *"Joe never quit anything without creating some kind of 'win' first. He was always able to extract some kind of value out of every situation..."*

Leon learned never to be frivolous about his time and his work—he'd make a firm **commitment** to put in the work necessary to get the job done. He also developed an attitude about each new position or role. He learned how to dive in with both feet and learn as **MUCH** as he could, as **FAST** as he could!

> *"Leon learned never to be frivolous about his time*
> *and his work—he'd make a firm commitment to*
> *put in the work necessary to get the job done."*

In a parallel universe, both Leon and Joe learned the craft of leadership well, but one thing ate away at both of them—it was their biggest challenge to overcome. Both men had a nagging problem with those people who had poor work ethics.

It drove both of them a little crazy!

Of course, over many years of leadership, both men had learned that you can lead a salesperson to water, but you can't force them to drink it. As they began to compare notes for the work that went into this chapter, they recognized that they'd each taken inventory of the words, thoughts and actions that may be indicative of a person who is planning to DO THE WORK and one that is NOT.

> *"...You can lead a salesperson to water, but*
> *you can't force them to drink it."*

Leon and Joe believe that these common threads have a habit of **announcing** themselves early in a salesperson's career and this singularity has been proven out in hundreds of people they have personally hired and trained. So the hypothesis here is that if a person is thinking, saying or doing certain things, those factors become **predictors** of whether they are going to do the work or not. Another way to look at this is that these traits easily form a profile or persona of the people that either fail to launch, or the opposite, they become a rock star.

> *"So the hypothesis here is that if a person is thinking, saying*
> *or doing certain things, those factors become predictors*
> *of whether they are going to do the work or not."*

While the following notes are less a scientific behavioral analysis, than simply **informal observations**, we think you'll find these traits quite helpful in identifying what may exist **inside** of yourself or others. Hence these traits can be forecasters of who may be ready to show up and do the work.

FAILURES TO LAUNCH (Markers of salespeople who DON'T show up and do the work)

We've listed a number of characteristics, thoughts and actions of those salespeople that typically **don't do the work** and subsequently wash out of the organizations they are in:

- *Lack of **discipline** (Both personally and professionally)*
- ***Poor** habits regarding **follow-up** on leads and opportunities (A real red flare)*
- *An apparent lack of **self-confidence***
- ***Not punctual** for meetings, appointments, etc. (Late or no show)*
- ***Bad conversationalist** (Not able to further a casual dialog)*
- *Doesn't ask **questions** (Not curious)*
- *Little **engagement** (At training or meetings)*
- *Doesn't ask for **help***
- ***Loner** tendencies*
- *Becomes **distracted** easily*
- *Flustered or crushed by any **push back***
- *Unable to **recognize** what went wrong*

It may seem that we've just described the worst prospective salesperson ever. The point of this exercise is to have each reader, whether they're an entry-level salesperson or an experienced sales trainer, become cognizant of these characteristics. These tendencies are forecasters of a person that **isn't completely committed to the work**.

If you're a newer salesperson, the operative question would be, "Do I recognize any of these traits in myself?" In the event that you're a trainer, we would challenge you to become cognizant of these indicators and monitor which salespeople you can influence and which you cannot. We believe that a newer salesperson can identify any singular item that may be an issue and fix it. If they are OPEN, they can ask for help from their manager, trainer or coach and get back to doing the work.

FUTURE ROCK STARS (Indicators of salespeople who will show up and commit to the work)

Now, for the flip side—we'll list a number of traits that are highly indicative of those that **will go to work** and stick and stay in sales:

- *Highly **dependable** (Does what they say they're going to do)*
- *Great with **follow through** on leads and opportunities*
- *Shows a **confident** face (Even if they have to fake it til' they make it)*
- ***On time** (even early) for meetings and appointments*
- *Able to **engage** easily (With prospects, managers, peers, etc.)*
- *Asks **questions** incessantly (They are **curious** people)*
- *Willing to ask for **help** (Very open to what they don't know)*
- *These salespeople want to be part of a **high-functioning team***
- *They **stay focused***
- *They have a **thick skin***
- *Able to **recognize** what went wrong (As it's going wrong)*

The list above is a 'dream' for most sales managers, trainers and coaches. We don't always get this entire package...typically; we're ecstatic if we get **half** of these traits announcing themselves.

The objective behind these two contrary lists of characteristics is to get you thinking about what persona of salesperson typically **does the work** and what profile usually **doesn't show up** to do the work. Of course, this is a book designed to encourage a salesperson to **ADOPT** and practice attitudes and mindsets that **winning salespeople** all practice. So we're hopeful that you'll use this chapter lesson to form your own mindsets regarding the work. If you take nothing away from this brief lesson chapter we hope that these takeaways come through:

There are few mindsets MORE important than those surrounding your work ethic and how you value the work

The mindsets behind going to work aren't natural attributes; they're simply a choice that you will make

Our belief is that you can actually choose to ADOPT any or all of the rock star traits. These characteristics can help you intentionally remove any roadblock that may stand in the way of picking up the phone or walking into a business. We've learned how to **show up** everyday, ready to go to work on our craft, with a smile on our face. That's how success and wealth are developed in sales.

Are you **showing up**?

CHAPTER 16

The Vision-Reality Bridge

Connecting dreams to execution
+ accomplishment

KATIE ANDERSON WITH JOE BUZZELLO

*"Ideas are easy. It's the **execution** of ideas that*
really separates the sheep from the goats."

—SUE GRAFTON

We often hear leaders speak of the word "Vision". Some are fanatical about it. They write the word in BIG LETTERS on the board and ask each member of the team to announce their own individual vision and purpose. They also ask salespeople to buy-in to the team's big picture objective. Salespeople tear apart magazines creating elaborate "vi-

119

sion boards" rallying around the rah rah of their carefully crafted (and conspicuously displayed) dreams.

It all sounds good. And it is good.

An individual should—we'll even say **MUST**—have a crystalized idea of where they want to take their career. A big and compelling vision is necessary, it's exciting, it drives energy...it can even drive higher levels of activity, but there's a potential (and common) problem with all of this vigor. We often get so wrapped up in the excitement of what we're told we can build, that we forget that all of our fabulous dreams depicted on that vision board can only come to fruition if we cross the bridge from **vision** to **reality**—the reality that's wrapped up and hidden inside of the necessary day-to-day execution of the right activities in the right volume.

> *"...All of our fabulous dreams depicted on that vision board can only come to fruition if we cross the bridge from vision to reality..."*

There are a lot of reasons salespeople may crash and burn. There are dozens of excuses we can expertly craft, however, the hard truth is that direct sales—especially commission-based—is just not that easy!

We must identify that there are inherent challenges that make this game tough—trials such as:

- *Constant **failure***
- *Massive **rejection***
- *Continuous **distractions***
- *Poor training*
- *Little or no **structure***
- *A need for constant **self-discipline***

Because of these real-world factors and countless others, it's imperative that we steer clear of the nasty habit of **making excuses** and we practice two other critical doctrines:

1. We must create a **BIG, CLEAR vision** for ourselves

2. We have to *cross* the **BRIDGE** between our vision and the **RE-ALITY** of what it will take to get the job done

If we don't ADOPT the two beliefs listed above, our road in sales is destined to meet a swift dead end. Let's go deeper for a moment on the "crash and burn" thing. What goes on in the real world of commission sales and solo-preneurship? Why is there so much carnage?

The truthful answer to that question lies between the "C" and the "A" inside of **The CAP Equation**˙ sales methodology. We need to learn how to develop a strong vision, which is a "Competency." In addition, we will need to foster the mindset or "Attitude" that we'll stay **rooted in the reality** of what it takes to cross the bridge to sustained success. Far too often we see people trapped in one of two categories, both of which can prove **fatal** in the sales world.

All Talk – No Heart

These are lovely people—so positive coming out of training school. They're big picture raconteurs and they can **dream build** until the cows come home. However, there's one small problem with these folks...they lack a **connection** to reality. There is an absence of understanding (or recognition) of what it actually *takes* to get to the **Promised Land**. They're missing the heart to suck it up and do the work necessary.

Grinder Without A Cause

Our second category is populated with fine people that actually know how to **grind it out** on a day-to-day basis. They're field warriors that DO show up and go to work. On the surface these people look like a gift from the heavens for any sales manager; however, they're lacking a strong codified vision—a **reason, purpose** or **cause**—one strong enough to sustain them through the tough times that will surely arise. They eventually run themselves ragged. Without a strong vision they're merely running on a hamster wheel, hoping for the best, but unable to finish the race when their emotional gas tank empties. They eventually ask, "Why in the heck am I doing this?"

These are definitely two **different** personas, but in the end, both types lose the war. The big picture, "All Talk – No Heart" guy will never achieve the results necessary to see their utopian vision come to fruition. They simply don't have a dialed-in work ethic that's based on the knowledge and reality of what it will take to succeed in sales.

Conversely...

The "Grinder Without A Cause" will fall to the wayside despite worn out shoes and a hoarse voice. They'll inevitably **burn out** because they lack a strong, internal long-term vision to hang onto.

> *Neither of these types have built a BRIDGE from a strong vision to the stark reality of things, and then learned how to cross it!*

How do we become the sales professional that effectively builds our bridge from a big picture **visionary** to a calendar cadenced **workhorse**, one who's able to navigate the challenges of a life in commission sales? It happens when we first practice the **crafting** of a strong, **codified vision**, and also **fiercely commit** to an attitude that helps us cross over that bridge so that we can make our dreams a reality.

A GREAT EXAMPLE

We've certainly observed the professionals that *crossed* the bridge and also helped others do so. There's a leader that embodies the mindset and attitudes we're referring to in this chapter.

Lisa Hall worked with a Fortune 500' company for several decades. She was the consummate sales professional, and a highly motivated leader of leaders. She grossed seven-figures in personal income for many years. Lisa was able to cross back and forth between the **vision** and **reality** thing better than most. She held two **ardent beliefs** in her head at one time as she was on-boarding new eager salespeople:

1. New people needed to **SEE** and **FEEL** the **BIG PICTURE**
2. They needed to jump **INTO** the **WEEDS** and make things happen

Lisa made sure that both of the ends of the spectrum met in the **middle** of the bridge. She'd move back and forth in this "bridge" mentality so that her team could more easily understand the work that would be necessary to stay on target for what they wished to accomplish.

When asked about her philosophies in this area, Lisa would say, "I simply stay aware of **what's actually happening** in the field. It's my job to cast the **big vision** without losing sight of the **actual work** that needs to happen to get us there."

> *"I simply try to stay AWARE of what's actually happening in the field. It's my job to help cast the big vision without losing sight of the actual WORK that needs to happen to get us there."*

Lisa was an amazing leader—casting a **big vision**—one that her entire team rallied behind, however, the team never lost sight of the **reality** of the work that it would take. She stayed **connected** to what the game was *actually* like in the field and what the work felt like.

Lisa also practiced some other mindsets that she passed onto her team. She believed that a person should:

- *Be in constant reflection of where they're REALLY at*
- *Seek coaching on the activity levels necessary (to meet goals)*
- *Make small navigational tweaks when needed*

Like all great salespeople and sales leaders, Lisa believed that you should do these three things proactively and often:

1. **Assess** *(Where am I right now?)*
2. **Re-assess** *(Are my actions moving me closer to my stated goals?)*
3. **Re-group** *(What new strategies/resources do I need?)*

Lisa had strong mindsets in the area of vision, goal setting and the reality of making it all come to pass. She wouldn't throw out **arbitrary numbers** without determining how the team could actually get there.

Breaking Down The Mindset

This attitude is not a complex one. There are only three pieces of this mindset and practice:

1. The **Vision**
2. The **Reality**
3. The **Bridge**

Let's first take a look at the mindset and attitudes that constitute a strong vision.

The Vision:

We could dedicate hundreds of pages to the subject of **vision**, what it is, how it works, how it fails, how to sell it, etc., but for the sake of focus, we're simply going to offer a few pertinent questions. You may wish to jot down some thoughts based on the following prompts:

- *What's important to you NOW?*
- *What do you need to do/provide for your FAMILY?*
- *How much MONEY would you like to earn?*
- *What's important to you in the FUTURE?*
- *What is it that you want to BUILD?*
- *What would you like to BECOME?*

When you look at your needs and wants, what jumps out at you? How do you want to change your lifestyle? What are your family needs—owning a home...bigger home...kids in college...taking care of aging parents? What's the next significant level of income you'd like to earn? Where do you wish to be in 2, 5 or 10 years? What kind of business are you trying to build? What do you wish to become in the process? What type of personal or spiritual growth would you like to pursue?

As you can see, the vision you create can be many-faceted. It will require thought and work. We take a moment to also mention what a personal vision should **BE** for you.

It **SHOULD** be:

- Enduring
- Compelling
- Clear

We're suggesting your vision should be **durable**, stable and lasting. It must survive the struggles you'll have. It should also be **compelling**—convincing you that it's more worthy than **giving up**. Finally, your vision must be **clear**. Your vision must form a vibrant picture in your mind. This type of attractive vision will enable you to re-fill your emotional gas tank over and over again.

We are also obliged to tell you what a vision shouldn't or can't be.

It **CAN'T** be:

- Weak or haphazard or fleeting
- Unexciting
- Muddy

Bottom line, if you don't spend the proper time and thought on the formation of your vision, it will be **fragile**, **uninteresting** and **murky**. It will have no power or influence over you. You may grind it out for a while, only to fall short of what you've told everyone you wish to accomplish.

The Reality:

A grand vision can be enough to *motivate* us to a **certain point**, but unless we develop the **willingness** to dive into **the weeds**, it all becomes just a nice fairytale. Salespeople that aren't **in touch** with the day-to-day realities of the **WORK** will struggle, and then die.

Here's a short list of the 4 **realities of the work** that you'll have to form belief systems around:

- Your willingness to **DO** the work *(Your 10,000 hours)*
- Your desire to **HONOR** the work *(Doing the work well with pride)*

- Knowing exactly what **VOLUME** of work is required *(Activity levels)*

Your understanding of what the work will **FEEL** like *(On an emotional level)*

Let's unpack this **WORK** thing a bit more.

First, if a person is going to survive in commission sales, they have to be 100% **WILLING** to **DO** the **WORK**. Without that foundational attitude a person is sunk before they begin. They must be willing to invest 10,000 hours to become a master at their craft.

If you aren't aware of this "10,000-hour" thing, Malcolm Gladwell wrote about it in his 2008 book, Outliers. Gladwell claims that greatness requires time, perhaps about 10,000 hours. Some challenge this hypothesis, but we like it because it is a recognizable benchmark (or tangible number) that we've seen play out to be somewhat accurate.

Simply asked, are you willing to put in your 10,000 hours?

We'd like to go one step further, suggesting that all top performers not only put in their 10,000-hours, but they also **HONOR** the work—striving to do the **BEST work possible**—improving on their craft every day.

Let's move onto the third bullet point—recognizing the **VOLUME** of work necessary, and chunking that down into something that can be **executed** and measured each day and week. We will admit that this element may sound like a **Pipeline Practice** (The "P" in the CAP Equation or even like a "C", Competency); however, it's a mindset first. Pros first commit to **knowing their numbers** and metrics at all times.

The last element of the four **realities of the work** is about the control of one's **emotions**—what the work **FEELS** like as you grind away, but see no tangible results. The mindset you must establish in this area is about **the long haul**—finishing the race. You acknowledge that you'll have to pump the pump for a certain period of time before water begins to dribble out and then flow freely. A long-term thinking mindset must be forged.

So the **reality** of things is that a lot of work will be necessary for you to reach your stated objectives. You'll need to settle on some very strong and supportive attitudes around that work.

The Bridge:

You've learned that **vision** without an awareness of **reality** is a complete waste of time...and vice versa. You've probably also figured out that **both** vision and a sense of reality can exist, but without a **link** between the two, a **disconnect** will occur and you'll crash and burn just the same. An unwavering sense of **purpose** + your **connection** to a firm **commitment** to the work **IS** your **BRIDGE** to sustained success.

> *"An unwavering sense of purpose + your connection to a firm commitment to the work IS your BRIDGE to sustained success."*

The Vision-Reality Bridge is a mindset that (in some form) ALL high-level salespeople and sales leaders practice. They may not even know how to describe it or articulate it. This is a common thing for many high performers. We've simply taken the opportunity to expound on this attitude for you in this chapter.

Before we wrap this chapter up and place a bow on it, we want you to focus on a couple of the words in the large word text above:

PURPOSE–CONNECTION–COMMITMENT–WORK

The best and the brightest sales and entrepreneurial rock stars have a rock solid (and clear) **PURPOSE**. They're constantly *recalling* that purpose and **CONNECTING** it to their daily **COMMITMENT**—vigilance to the **WORK** they know is essential and necessary to their success. So the people that kill it keep these things **top of mind** and **close** to their **heart**. They are masterful at **bridging** their **vision** to the **reality** of the work. They know that the work has to happen—no excuses! They honor the work—want to get better at it each day. They know their metrics well. They are good at monitoring their **emotions**.

Pros travel back and forth across the Vision/Reality Bridge every day. There is no separation between where they wish to **GO** and **HOW** they know they're going to get there. These two things are **FUSED**.

> ### *"Pros travel back and forth ACROSS the Vision/Reality Bridge every day. There is no separation between where they wish to GO and HOW they know they're going to get there. These two things are FUSED."*

So there you have it!

Bottom line...few people will stay with a commission sales organization (or any venture) long-term if they don't have a strong **vision**. If they're lucky they'll have a leader who casts a big vision, but ultimately, their own (personal) vision will be the one that sustains them. Conversely, a strong vision can paint a picture, but "talk is cheap" and the dream will only buoy them for a short time.

You have an important decision to make in your sales career.

Will you be **ALL Talk**—and light on the work? Or...are you going to be the "**Grinder**" that does the work, but doesn't go deep, creating a compelling set of dreams?

We obviously want you to be the person who **CONNECTS** those two things, vision + reality—walking freely across the bridge, knowing where you want to **GO** and also knowing exactly **HOW you're going to get there**.

The choice is yours, but if you're reading this book; we think we know what **mindset decision** you've already made! ☺

CHAPTER 17

Accountability to Yourself FIRST

Taking 100% ownership of your career

JOE BUZZELLO

*"Life is not accountable to us. We are **accountable** to life."*
—DENIS WAITLEY

I believe that an attitude of 100% **personal** accountability and responsibility might be the greatest differentiator between success and failure for the NEWEST salesperson. However, I've observed that accountability is one of those things that some ignore. I have also noticed that some simply **hope** that a sense of accountability will **magically appear**—without conscious work.

But accountability just doesn't *happen*!

Personal responsibility is something that has to be fostered and worked on, 24/7. You have to have a clear and consistent strategy of how you are going to **implement** it and **validate** it for yourself. Of course, it starts and ends with YOU, and it has to *apply* at all times. We will also point out that becoming personally accountable for your career—taking ownership of it **first**—is far <u>more powerful</u> than someone from above you **pushing it down**—mandating it.

> ### *"Personal responsibility is something that has to be fostered and worked on, 24/7."*

If you are **dependent** on someone else for your accountability, it means that you have not yet developed or strengthened an ability to *govern* your own thoughts, emotions, attitudes, and work habits. In other words, you're nothing more than somebody that possesses an "employee mentality". The first time your hierarchy isn't there to hold your feet to the fire, or wipe your nose, or dry your tears, you'll revert to all of your own irresponsible ways.

That sounds like a fairly **weak** stance, doesn't it?

It's definitely not the place we want you to be in. We want you to learn how to become accountable to yourself FIRST, before you expect or ask **anybody else** to hold you accountable. We want you to develop an attitude that moves you to take **complete ownership** of your career, before you ever get started. That's what this chapter is about.

Learning to Work in Isolation

A few of us old cronies have this sarcastic little saying. It pops up in random texts once in a while.

"I feel isolated and lonely in my daily activities!"

I don't think that any of us that have taken a few trips around the sun in sales hasn't felt this way. It's just that real hardcore pros have learned how to **self-govern** during these moods. I certainly felt isolated when I began to sell insurance (on a commission-only basis) at the tender age of eighteen. My first outside sales gig involved selling accident insurance to business owners for Pennsylvania Life. The work was mostly cold calling—walking into small businesses. After completing all of their basic classroom training—and a few days in the field with my trainer—I went solo—was completely **alone** in my work.

It was brutal!

Just imagine an eighteen-year-old kid, armed with nothing more than a sight seller, some instant issue policies and a memorized pitch. Oh...and there was one other thing I was armed with.

They gave us a pack of index-sized cards. The numbers 1 – 60 were printed on the card—the goal being to walk into a total of sixty doors each workday. The card looked like this:

Countdown to Success									
1	2	3	4	5	6	7	8	9	10
11	12	13	14	15	16	17	18	19	20
21	22	23	24	25	26	27	28	29	30
31	32	33	34	35	36	37	38	39	40
41	42	43	44	45	46	47	48	49	50
51	52	53	44	55	56	57	58	59	60

I was instructed to place one fresh *Countdown to Success* card in my shirt pocket at the start of each day. I was told to *cross off* a number each time I walked into a door. You were to *circle* the number if the business owner allowed you to give them a full presentation. If you were able to make a sale, you would write down the number of "units" of business you sold next to the circle.

With this simple tool, they were prompting us to walk into sixty doors a day. They knew that if you **stayed accountable** to that **magic number** of walk-ins, good things would happen.

They told me that if I walked into sixty doors a day, 12 – 15 business owners would stop and listen to me. That part sounded good, but what I didn't immediately realize is that this also meant that 45 – 48 people would ask me to leave their shop! Of the 12 – 15 that would listen to our pitch, they estimated that 3 – 5 of them would purchase 7 – 10 units of business. This would all equate to a sales agent making a decent living in 1982, which was about $100–$150 a day.

Their numbers DID work.

But you had to be **accountable** to them!

To be honest, I didn't totally get the *Countdown to Success* cards at first. I didn't use them right away. I also didn't have much success right away. I made 12 – 15 walk-ins my first day as a solo dude. I don't think I even topped 20 walk-ins any day during my first week. My second week didn't go much better, and then I had that impactful conversation with my dad—the one where I told him that I was thinking of quitting. If you read that story in my first book, *The CAP Equation*, you will recall that my father, Buzz, simply challenged me to become accountable to the numbers that they believed worked. He told me that I should "Use those 'Countdown' cards they gave you." He advised me to, "Prove their numbers wrong." My dad was inspiring me to become accountable to **myself**, but it seemed easier for me to simply become accountable to those 60 numbers on those dumb index cards.

> *"My dad was inspiring me to become accountable to myself, but it seemed easier for me to simply become accountable to those 60 numbers on those dumb index cards."*

That conversation with my dad was a **turning point** in my thinking and my attitude. I made the decision to at least become accountable to something. The next week (my third full week in the field) was much better. While I didn't hit the magic number of 60 every day, I hit that number most days. From the fourth week on I was totally accountable to those *Countdown to Success* cards.

Those cards became my accountability partner!

> *"I made the decision to at least become accountable to something."*

The weird thing is, I thought I was being accountable to the index cards or the numbers on them, but so much more was happening. I was systematically training myself to be **accountable to myself** while working in isolation. To some degree, all of us are going to have to learn how to work successfully in isolation. Your sales position may require you to make cold calls or follow-up visits in the field, or it may consist of doing a great deal of phone work. You may have someone supporting you for a small percentage of your work-day; however, I'm assuming that a larger percentage of your selling time will be spent alone. It's during those periods of time that you must practice total personal accountability and take complete ownership of your career.

> *"...A larger percentage of your selling time will be spent alone. It's during those periods of time that you must practice total personal accountability and take complete ownership of your career."*

During my first month in sales I was fortunate enough to figure some essential things out.

What I learned was:

- *Outside sales can be a **lonely** place*
- *Nobody is going to **force** you to put in a **full day** and effort*
- *You must become **accountable to something**—fast!*
- *The **best person** (or thing) to be accountable to is **YOURSELF**!*

While I didn't enter the game with a well-formed personal accountability and career ownership mindset, I quickly figured out that **one would be required** if I was going to stick and stay in sales. I also soon learned that if you do become personally accountable to the work, activities and efforts, then many other great benefits and resources appear.

WHAT PERSONAL ACCOUNTABILITY (OR A LACK OF IT) MEANS

As I progressed past the first few months in my sales career into my second year and beyond, the benefits and meaning of **taking ownership** of one's career became clear to me. I was also able to identify who was going to make it long-term and who would be a flameout. As I matured in my career I was able to form some key opinions about this thing we call "accountability". A few **poignant lessons** announced themselves to me that I began to form and establish attitudes and mindsets on.

Here are just a few of my observations:

- Whether they tell you this or not, as a commission salesperson, personal accountability is an **integral part** of the job description.
- If you try to **duck personal accountability** it will have a swift and negative impact on your results.
- You are responsible (and must stand accountable) for **everything that happens** inside of your career.
- Accountability and ownership is not a "sometimes" thing; it's an **all-the-time** thing! You can't just be accountable when it's comfortable.
- Salespeople, who don't want to be held accountable, are always looking for any opportunities **(excuses)** to *get out of* things.
- The only way to **stay** accountable is to set yourself up for success. You must have **all the tools**. (Nobody's going to take ownership of something they believe is going to fail)
- Some people never act accountable, and when things start to go awry, they go into **spectator mode** and watch as their venture fails.
- If they thought they would *fail* from the **outset** it's even worse; they go into, "I told you so" mode, which nearly always becomes a self-fulfilling prophecy.
- When people **DO take ownership** (and if things start to go wrong), they typically step into **solution mode**. They figure out what's going on and they fix it.
- When salespeople come into the game with an **entitlement mindset** (everyone needs to be accountable to me) they are doomed for failure from the start.

If you're new in sales (or if you've been around a while), but not killing it, you have a decision to make. You will have to decide if you are mature enough to take responsibility over yourself. There is definitely an option...you can certainly shun any personal responsibility—you can wait for someone else to "motivate" you to go to work—but life doesn't work that way.

A great motivational legend, and a person I had the pleasure of meeting at a young age, Denis Waitley, said, "Life is not accountable to us. We are accountable to life." With that quote, Denis is implying that life isn't going to drop great stuff into your lap as you wait around. You are going to have to be accountable to your dreams, desires and objectives first. Then good things will happen.

I believe that those of us that **get that** do very well from the inception of our careers. I was so fortunate as to have been handed a stack of those wonderful little *Countdown to Success* index cards in 1982, and then my dad tricked me into actually being accountable to them. I formed a habit of being personally responsible and that great habit has lasted over four decades.

The **decision** to take ownership of my career came first. I know that if you'll simply make the decision to become personally accountable to yourself, and resolve to take complete ownership of your career, then **great things can happen...*and they often do!***

SECTION 5

Emotional Controls, Humility + Self Talk

*Seeking **prosperity**, becoming other-centered, practicing **humility** and controlling the **voices** in your own head.*

CHAPTER 18

A Prosperity Mindset

Choosing abundance

BRANDEE JUSTUS WITH JOE BUZZELLO

*"I chose not to **identify** with being broke any longer. I realized I deserved a beautiful life, and **abundance** was something that I needed to welcome into my life."*

—JEN SINCERO

You can spot it a mile away! It's easy if you've spent years coaching commission salespeople. We're talking about **contrary** mindsets.

We often celebrate the end of someone's first **solo** field day with a quick meeting. Sometimes, we'll have two people that started at the same time, and this makes a party of three to recap the day. We'll call our two newbies Chad and Sue. Chad was a young, professional looking guy in his late twenties. He had huge financial goals—told Brandee that he was going to, "kill it" when she hired him. Sue was studious—right out of college. She was friendly, but had an edge that told you she was all business.

When Brandee arrived, Chad was waiting. He looked tired and distraught. When she sat down he blurted out that he'd walked into twenty-six doors and, "Everyone has already seen our plans." He was only two weeks into his new career and convinced that the salespeople that had worked the area had "already scooped up" all of the "good accounts". He went so far as to wonder, out loud, "Why did you guys even hire me?"

Brandee pressed him for accuracy on his numbers. She quickly learned that he'd only spoken to four decision makers. One asked him to follow up in two weeks. The second didn't own our plans, but Chad wasn't able to engage with him enough to schedule a meeting. The last two leads were working with a competitor. Coincidentally, those two companies were located in the same building of that competitor.

It was apparent to Brandee that Chad was so focused on the three companies that didn't seem to be available to him that he was blind to the fact that the other twenty-two places he'd called on were still opportunities for him.

Bottom line...Chad was mired in what we call a **poverty** mindset.

Conversely, when Sue arrived, she told Brandee that she had popped into over thirty businesses. She'd spoken to nine decision makers and had set two appointments. Sue referred back to her notes and told Brandee that she also had three follow-ups, and four definite NO's. She was excited about the upcoming appointments, but also thrilled that she'd gained some 'intel' about the companies where a decision maker wasn't immediately available.

Think about it...Sue had made a **conscious decision** to learn as much as she could about her prospects so that her next follow-up with them could be even more effective. Sue was stoked to have identified additional companies that weren't on her original leads list. Her instincts were telling her, "The more you look around, the more leads you can add to your list!"

Sue was operating from a place of **possibility**—what we refer to as a **prosperity** mindset.

I think you get the point of this very real (and all too common) illustration. Your outlook—how you **perceive** a set of circumstances—is a major factor in the formation of your attitude as a professional salesperson. Your results (good or bad) will follow along that very same path.

> *"Your outlook—how you perceive a set of circumstances—is a major factor in your attitude as a professional salesperson. Your results (good or bad) will follow along that very same path."*

When a true sales professional **owns** his or her attitude, they operate from a belief in **prosperity**—that good things are going to happen. Of course, the opposite occurs when one views that they are facing **scarcity**. Typically, those with a prosperous outlook are grounded and secure. They see the **BIG picture** and understand the cycle of sales. On the contrary, those that interpret life through a lens of poverty live or die with every approach and each micro result. As a consequence of that mindset, when they finally do have an opportunity in front of them, they can't see it.

PROSPERITY + PROSPECTING (MORE EXAMPLES USING SUE AND CHAD)

Prospecting is an area where prosperity verses poverty mindsets are easy to identify. It's a coach's responsibility to help new people build their prospect list. We start by supplying raw data, but after scrubbing, we're often left with fifty percent of the initial list. Right away, you can spot those folks who have a prosperity mindset. They use the initial list as a starting point only—**adding to it** based on personal contacts and knowledge of the local market. They're willing to take what's offered and immediately expand on it to create **more opportunity** for themselves.

Then, there's the other kind of mindset...

This is the **poverty** mindset on display—these folks never build on the initial list. They burn through their initial leads—making only a half-hearted, one-time pass. Then they come running back for more leads. They don't look around, observing and adding other prospects to their list—prospects that are (literally) right in their path. They're shocked that other salespeople may have called on leads that came from a public database. LOL! They're operating from a sense of **entitlement** and also a poverty mindset.

Most people will agree that prospecting is a tough thing. You are interrupting someone's day, attempting to divert their attention to what **you believe** should be important to them. Of course, your mindset going into a day of cold calling dramatically impacts your results.

Sue believed she could **positively** influence someone's day by delivering her carefully crafted message. As a result, she consistently set quality appointments. Sue's prosperity mindset positioned her as a successful salesperson—the type of person that buyers want to do business with. Sue won over many more prospects than someone with a dismal disposition.

Chad often has to cut his day short because, "Everyone was in a bad mood today". His poverty mindset doesn't allow him to visualize that he can have a positive affect on someone's day. He consistently allows others to control his attitude and activity level. This mindset drains energy and internal motivation quickly.

Each day there are salespeople that stop one approach short of greatness. It's that one call that could change their week, quarter or career. This occurs because they don't believe they can change their path for the day. In reality, a poverty mindset causes a person to believe that they can't control their path or career at all.

The person that lives in a **prosperous** world believes that they're solving problems for their customers and they reflect a position of **ingenuity**. Prosperous thinkers view their marketplaces as farmland that will continuously produce a fruitful harvest. They understand that each crop requires its own perfect mix of sunlight, water and fertilizer and are willing to adjust the formula for each individual plant.

Conversely, those with a poverty mindset are not concerned with providing value to their prospect or customer. Unfortunately, they're focused on **personal needs** and that elusive **next sale**. They can damage the marketplace and often drive their customers away with a self-centered approach.

When a salesperson operates in this **poverty mindset** manner, we believe it speaks to a short-term thinking mentality. They are unwilling to see things from any perspective other than that which they believe to be the most immediately profitable. It's all about here and now.

Let's look at a few stark examples of the **diverse** attitudes:

Prosperity Mindset		Poverty Mindset
I create my own opportunities		I am entitled to...
There are endless possibilities	**Vs.**	The market is saturated
I can change someone's day today		Everyone's in a bad mood today
I want to solve problems for people		I need to make a sale

To further illustrate what can occur when a mindset is faulty...

Chad and Brandee worked together on a prospect for over four months. They had multiple meetings and there was a crazy amount of correspondence needed to overcome multiple objections. Brandee recalls leaving the meeting where they finally got a **YES**. Brandee was on cloud nine after this WIN, but as they got into the car, Chad said, "We will see if this sticks". Brandee was floored when Chad described the win as a "fluke."

It wouldn't have been appropriate for Brandee to say what she was thinking. LOL! Instead, she reviewed each step taken to get the deal closed. She emphasized that **patience** had been on their side. Brandee advised Chad that because they had covered so much ground with **transparency**, a great deal of trust had been established. Brandee also commented that she expected the relationship to become stronger—anticipating many recommendations/referrals coming to them. Chad thought that Brandee was "getting carried away" and commented that he believed Brandee was, "expecting too much." Bottom line, Chad had little recognition of future opportunities because of his poverty mindset.

It is our belief that if you consistently do the work (and **honor** the work), your business will grow, however, there's a glaring difference between **incremental growth** and **great prosperity**. To truly prosper in your business, you must EXPECT that things will go your way. Those with a prosperous mindset typically strive to become trusted partners with their customers, positively impacting as many facets of their operations as possible. They must be willing to go the extra mile.

Alternatively, a poverty mindset reflects an attitude of...

"...If I can't make a commission, it's not my job."

That disposition makes quality relationships impossible and yields only short-term customers, if any come to you at all!

It shouldn't surprise you that, by most standards, those with a mindset of prosperity are typically viewed as better **teammates**. They're more **collaborative** and believe that success for each yields success for all. They see opportunity in everything because they view the marketplace as vast and open, they don't feel threatened when others excel.

Conversely, those with a poverty mindset are **hoarders** of success. This often causes them to be hesitant to share their wins (and best practices) fearing their teammates will steal not only their glory, but also their opportunities.

The next time you're in a sales meeting we challenge you to observe your teammates' behaviors. You'll find that those that reflect a prosperous mindset are not only the favorites of the group, but they're more financially successful as well.

"You'll find that those that reflect a prosperous mindset are not only the favorites of the group, but they're more financially successful as well."

At some point in your life, someone has probably said to you...

"I can't promise you it will be easy, however, I can promise you it will be well worth it."

This is what we would say to you about *adopting* a prosperity mindset. Human nature leads us to skepticism, especially when we're following an **unconventional** path. We believe it's also natural for people to take the path of **least resistance**. In sales, what often appears to be the easiest route is not the most beneficial in the long term. The most successful commission sales professionals are conscious of their attitudes at all times. A prosperity mindset reflects that **without challenges**, victory would never be as sweet and embraces the opportunity to learn from setbacks.

We'd like to WRAP up this chapter with one last example...

...An example of what happens when you keep your eyes and heart open, and you have a firm belief in your ability to create success.

The young man came from humble beginnings, but had natural entrepreneurial instincts. In middle school he sold garbage bags to earn money to buy the latest and greatest tennis shoes. In high school he graduated to selling coins and stamps. His loving parents let him dream, but also encouraged him to learn a trade as a "fall back" position.

The trades didn't work for the person in our example. He tried carpentry and food service—failing miserably at both. Undaunted, he registered for classes at Indiana University, but he never visited the school; he simply decided to attend because it was the highest-ranking business school he felt he could get into and afford the tuition for. To make ends meet, he gave dance lessons and hosted disco parties at the local National Guard facility.

Immediately following his time at Indiana, he suffered a disastrous entrepreneurial escapade. It was his first real venture—involving a powdered milk product. His new business faltered and tanked. But he didn't quit on his dreams. It would have been easy to slink his way out of the business world with his tail between his legs...but he didn't do that. He had a few other false starts, but by 1995 he'd built and sold his consulting business, Microsolutions, to CompuServe for $6,000,000.

Continuing to search for great opportunities, he and a college classmate, saw opportunity with the new World Wide Web. They started a company called AudioNet. The idea for the new company came from a desire to gain access to IU basketball games. Despite massive criticism of their business model during the early days, they continued to build and in just three years they were able to sell AudioNet to Yahoo for $6,000,000,000!

Of course, the young man we're talking about is **Mark Cuban**.

Mark Cuban purchased the Dallas Mavericks of the NBA in 2000. The team was on the skids and had not made the playoffs in more than a decade. Cuban used his prosperity mindset and the old adage, "If you build it they will come." He spoiled his players and erected a new stadium. Cuban's enthusiasm and will to win—to see the team prosper—was absolutely contagious. In 2001, the team had set a franchise record for wins and qualified for the playoffs. In 2006 they competed in the NBA finals and in 2011 they won the NBA Championship.

Make no mistake...Mark Cuban faced many challenges during his entrepreneurial journeys. He had been fired from several jobs, was unable to pay his bills at one point. He even had his lights turned off and a credit card cut up. His first television show was cancelled before it aired. He faced harsh critics at many junctures; however, he has always maintained a BIG picture view and a prosperity mindset. These tools prevented the temporary setbacks from becoming permanent walls.

> **"...He has always maintained a BIG picture view and a prosperity mindset. These tools prevented the temporary setbacks from becoming permanent walls."**

Cuban's **great attitude** propelled him FAR beyond the limitations that stopped most people he grew up with, went to school with and competed against in business. In sales and entrepreneurial pursuits, you can control two things, your **activity** and your **attitude**. It is imperative to take the time to exercise that control and approach each day with a view of prosperity.

Mark Cuban is just one example of what a **prosperous mindset** can do. It is powerful!

And you have a choice.

CHAPTER 19

Removing The DOLLAR Signs

(From your eyes)

RENEE CORSO WITH JOE BUZZELLO

*"Great salespeople are relationship builders who
provide **value** and help their customers win."*

—JEFFREY GITOMER

We can almost guarantee that you aren't going to sell **your stuff** in these current times the same way you sold your stuff back in the day. You won't be able to simply **show up** and survive, simply relying on your gifts of persuasion. It doesn't work that way anymore.

People are too smart—they have too much information about you and your products at their fingertips. You're going to have to be perceived by your buyer as being of **real value** to them.

We want to tell you about, Brent. (Not his real name)

He's typical of many people we might hire in sales. Like virtually all of us, he got into commission-based sales for the sick money you can make. He loved the fact that he could earn as much as he wanted. Nobody could hold him down. His objectives were to get to six figures in income as quickly as possible, and then earn **multiple** six figures.

It's all good—money is a potent motivator.

But there's also a challenge that often arises when somebody enters commission sales with dollar signs in their eyes. If they take that **singular mindset** out into the field, the people that they're trying to sell to will sense it—smell it—and they will run.

Our friend, Brent, dug into his new career, telling his manager that he was, "open, coachable," etcetera. He was also over-the-top competitive and he couldn't stop talking about the commissions he'd earn (and the awards he'd win) during his rookie year. He obsessed about his newfound abilities—the competencies he had learned in sales school—his ability to get appointments with decision makers when others couldn't. Brent was an appointment-making machine and he learned quickly how to close deals by watching his trainer make presentations during some initial meetings. It wasn't long before he was flying solo—trying to close his own deals. He had a little money in his pocket, but it wasn't quite enough.

So he began to press.

As he started to grind harder, his closing ratio went down. As his closing ratio went down, he resorted to even harder-edge closing techniques.

You get it...a vicious cycle.

While all this was going on, the voices inside of his head became louder and his outside voice became an issue. He'd say stuff like, "I couldn't 'nail' that one down. That one got away." It's as if he was going into each call with a mission to **take** something from each prospect instead of being curious about the prospect's position, and wondering what he could **give** to them. He was acting like a person who wanted to gain an edge on each person he met, versus simply **being of service**.

And isn't this exactly what people think most commission salespeople are all about—they're just out for a buck?

> *"It's as if he was going into each call with a mission to 'get something' from each prospect instead of being curious about the prospect's position and wondering what he could give to them."*

Brent needed to make a big shift.

He needed to get the dollar signs out of his eyes and focus his mindset on the real **mission** of a professional salesperson, but we'll get to that in a moment.

First, we want to share what one of Joe's early mentors did for him one day. Joe was short on cash, and a bit down in the dumps. His first sales manager, Tom, sensed a problem and grabbed Joe for a cup of coffee. It didn't take Tom long to figure out that Joe was low on funds and in a big, giant slump. As a result, Joe had started pressing. Each prospect was a target and every presentation became just a commission opportunity. This happened way back in 1979, when Joe was selling those $39 accident policies. Back then, a burger and fries cost less than $2.00. That sounds inexpensive, but Joe barely had $2.00 in his pocket.

He reluctantly mentioned this to Tom along with the fact that he felt it hard to focus on anything but a sale since he was so broke. Tom solved that problem. He reached into his own pocket and handed Joe a crisp hundred-dollar bill. He told Joe, "Here ya go. Now you're not broke any more. Fold this bill up and keep it in your wallet. Get the dollar signs out of your eyes and focus on how our accident plans help people pay their bills."

The rest of the story...

Joe went out in the field that day with a hundy in his Velcro wallet and a huge shift in his mindset. He didn't feel broke or desperate any longer. He heard Tom's message clearly—he relaxed and made the shift from what he could **GET**, to what he could **GIVE**. He killed it that day and the rest of that week. From that day forward he always had one or two crisp 'Benjamins' somewhere on his person, just so he never felt broke.

When Joe tells this story—even after forty years—you can see the twinkle in his eyes because it was one of those epiphany moments—a lesson frozen in time for him. He experienced a shift of **caring**. He went from worrying about when his next deal would close to actually caring about the prospect's position, needs, challenges and perceptions. The dollar signs that once occupied his eyes were gone. He went from *pretending* to care, to **actually** caring.

Although our friend, Brent, was offered the same kind of message and mentorship, he wasn't *ready* for the message. He never made the shift. As a result, he struggled until he washed out of the business of commission sales.

So there are a few big things going on here.

As a master sales coach, Renee likes to first identify where a person IS at—how much they've *evolved* in their life. If a person is just entering sales (and they plan to actually make it) she challenges them to get this mindset right. This mindset may feel foreign or even counterproductive.

Here are two big reasons:

Short Runway Mentality:

You're probably entering commission sales (or another gig) with a **limited runway** of cash in the bank. Your survival is about commission checks hitting your checking account after you close a few deals. So **the money** is going to be your natural focus. Closing deals will be top of mind versus building relationships, providing value or helping your prospects win.

Competitive Juices:

You may have joined an organization that features a competitive environment. If they're smart, they recognize you for what you've sold and the achievement levels you've reached on their ladder. It's all good, but again, this becomes about **the chase**. Your competitive juices kick in and you become focused on all of that bloodthirsty stuff instead of being focused on helping your prospect **solve problems** and experience a great outcome.

Don't take this advisement out of its intended context. We LOVE competitive salespeople, but **compartmentalization** has to happen when you step into the field—you must focus on a BETTER mission.

> ### *"We LOVE competitive salespeople, but some compartmentalization has to happen when you step into the field. You must focus on a BETTER mission."*

Money, revenue, recognition, awards, hearing your name called, being in the top ten or number one, it is all wonderful, but if you take that stuff out into the field and they sense you are not there to **hear** them and **serve** them, you're toast!

We want you to be able to sustain a career, have lots of gas in your tank, enjoy the heck out of what you're doing and serve people well. At the risk of being too esoteric, we wanted to throw out three of the other tremendous benefits of getting the dollar signs out of your eyes, besides just making more money.

1. *It allows you to RUN the LONG RACE*

Every part of this attitude feeds your ability to run the long race. When you're truly looking at your clients and asking, "What can I do to help them win," it removes virtually all of the stress that most people feel inside of their prior (flawed) sales process. **When stress is absent, energy and joy replace it**. We don't need a behavioral psychologist to tell us what happens when you have great energy and you are having fun in your chosen career.

2. *You do BETTER work (...and they refer you)*

We've never seen a salesperson make the shift we're referring to and NOT do better work as a result. We think the act of caring about creating true 'wins' for clients slows you down enough so that you don't miss all of the little things in the relationship that make a big difference. They perceive you as a top shelf salesperson and you're actually becoming one quickly. This, of course, also reflects itself in your stellar and growing reputation. It makes your clients want to refer you, again and again. In other words, **you are referable** in their eyes, when other people simply are not.

3. *Like the Grinch, your heart GROWS*

So if you make a decision to make this shift, you are actually **retraining your brain** to be a servant—to be of value to everyone you touch. As this shift occurs in your thoughts and then actions, you will find yourself enjoying the new you. You will wake up one morning and realize that what you're doing (and selling) is about so much more than simply pumping out nice commission checks. Over time, your eyes slowly shift from inward to **outward** and your heart for people and life becomes bigger.

> *"You will wake up one morning and realize that what you're doing (and selling) is about so much more than simply pumping out nice commission checks."*

Hopefully we're selling you on how **life-changing** this sales mindset can be, but in the odd chance we haven't, here's a quick list of characteristics/thoughts/comments we see and hear when the antithesis of this mindset exists: (People that can't or won't get the dollar signs out of their eyes)

- Fear Based Thinking

    · Afraid of NO
    · Afraid to "FAIL"
    · Afraid of what people are saying

- Low Activity Levels

    · Low energy
    · Cherry picking
    · Illness

- Shear Negativity

- "All prospects suck!"
- "It's someone else's fault I'm not making it" (victimized)
- "This work is too hard" (they're distracted)

People that can't or won't get the dollar signs out of their eyes, slowly stop showing up, and of course, they're automatically of **no use or value** to anyone in their marketplace. So if we've sold you on making the mindset shift of getting the dollar signs out of your eyes, we'd like to give you some thoughts of HOW to begin to make this shift or help others make it:

- It BEGINS and ENDS in your head

Making this caring 'thing' first in your head will require you to be **CONCIOUS** of it all of the time. It will be a 24/7 job until it becomes your norm.

- Come from a place of ABUNDANCE

You have to come from a place where you believe that there are so may good prospects for you out there that it doesn't matter who says **yes** or **no**.

- Think AMAZING

The shift happens when you realize (and adopt) that you have something **amazing** for them and it's simply your job to explain it (share it) with them and nothing more.

- Be PRESENT

When you're present on a sales call (phone or in person) it becomes about **them**, not you. You focus 100% on them.

- Trust your PROCESS

Do the work. Yeah, I know...too simple, right? If you focus on doing great work—messaging to people about how your products or services offer a solution or opportunity for them—a great outcome for them—then you have captured lightening in a bottle. So just do the work and trust the process and everything else will fall into place.

This is not rocket science, but on the other hand, it's not the easiest mindset to practice. However, we can assure you that once you get this one nailed down, a calmness will come over you because you will feel that you are doing amazing work for the people that are open to your message.

Like one of our mentors used to say, "We get to dress up in nice clothes, and then go tell nice people about our important products and services."

No stress there!

Decide to make this **attitude shift** today. You will be one giant step closer to building your legacy and your wealth.

CHAPTER 20

Being Intellectually Humble

The continued pursuit of wisdom

DAWN TYACK WITH JOE BUZZELLO

*"Humility is to make a **right** estimate of one's self!"*
—CHARLES SPURGEON

Humility.

On the surface, this may seem like an odd attitude to focus on. I'll agree that it's often overlooked, but we consider it a key mindset for your survival long-term.

Here's why...

You may have noticed someone who had some level of early success—and it went straight to his or her head. They may have entered the gig with an ego bigger than Rhode Island, or they may have been experiencing success for the first time—not really knowing how to process it. Regardless, the result is the same...they puff up...start thinking that they are 'hot stuff' and then they become shut down to the mentors that want to help them.

Even worse, many of us have had those managers that shout out orders with a red face and eyes bulging. They don't have time for "piss-ant" interjections or contradictions. They'll publicly belittle anyone that has a new thought or idea. They know what works and what doesn't, and they dislike being challenged. They fold their arms; prance around the office simply spouting off directives. These interesting folks wear their many years of experience like an exquisite badge of honor. Their ears are super-glued shut because of their "know-it-all" attitudes.

You know where we're going here.

Both of these human specimens don't (and can't) learn anything new. **They can't progress** past the point they're at. They have placed a self-imposed ceiling on their growth through their **blind** lack of humility. Their less-than-humble estimate of their own self worth is grossly inflated, and like a large, looming cloud, it blocks the sun—the warmth of knowledge and additional wisdom. Until these people return to a healthy place of **intellectual humility**, they will never gather any additional insights or grow professionally or personally.

> *"Until these people return to a healthy place of intellectual humility, they will never gather any additional insights or grow professionally or personally."*

We're not bagging on these folks for no good reason. They certainly do have degrees of experience, knowledge and wisdom, but they lack humility, and humility is the path to true self-development and enlightenment. We don't suggest this in a "Confucius" sort of way, but we suggest it based on the logic that if you are not humble, you are also typically not coachable.

Here's what the negative path may look like...

When a person has even a little success in business, they can begin to believe that they know everything about their industry and craft—that they have all the answers. As their triumphs build, they get further and further away from the foundation of their success, which was their coachability. They stop proactively and consciously adding tools to their knowledge base because their mind is no longer open. In fact, they can become downright unreceptive to new ideas and the consequence is the slow erosion of personal self-cultivation and growth.

These folks stagnate and become mostly irrelevant.

We know, this sounds gruesome and you don't ever think that this could describe you. We get it, but things like this can be subtle. We can find ourselves *vacillating* between healthy humility and unhealthy pride. It can be a slippery slope, or better yet, like walking on a tightrope. Strong, successful individuals learn how to identify the right balance between confidence in themselves (and their abilities), and the need to continue working on themselves. (Seeking mentorship from others)

> *"Strong, successful individuals learn how to identify the right balance between confidence in themselves (and their abilities), and the need to continue working on themselves. (Seeking mentorship from others)*

Let's not kid ourselves, there is always something **more to learn** and the top performers understand that none of us truly know the limits of our own abilities.

They stay open to the process.

At this point you still may be challenged by the concept of being both confident and relatively humble at the same time. On the surface it seems like these two words may be diametrically opposed to each other, however, we have learned that you can develop a beneficial attitude and mindset about this. You can be **confident** in yourself and your capabilities, but also be **humble** and grateful in your external communication and interactions with others. Most importantly, you can decide to remain open to new thoughts, ideas and feedback.

> *"You can be confident in yourself and your capabilities, but also be humble and grateful in your external communication and interactions with others."*

Elizabeth J. Krumrei-Mancuso, a professor of psychology at Pepperdine University, calls this **intellectual humility**. In her research, she details how those with high intellectual humility or awareness of their own fallibility exhibit more open-minded inquiry, more servant leadership, and less ideological polarization among other positive traits. She says:

> *"Without intellectual humility,*
> *we can't acquire new knowledge."*

We believe this last quote is critical for salespeople that are beginning to taste a bit of success. We know that if there's anything blocking your ability to acquire more knowledge, it can be a grave threat to your career.

Instead of that happening, we simply want you to create a thought process that places you in a position of **intellectual humility** so that you can continue to pursue and receive the wisdom and knowledge you will need to move to the next phase of your career.

CHAPTER 21

The Practice of Humility

...and the strength it provides a salesperson

KATIE ANDERSON WITH JOE BUZZELLO

"Humility, I have learned, must never be confused with meekness. Humility is being open to the ideas of others."

—SIMON SINEK

Humility is **NOT** humiliating.

This was an important language lesson for Katie as a child.

When she was a young girl, her father would talk with her about many concepts that some would deem, "over the head of a six-year old." One of these little talks revolved around the word, "humility." As a young person who was still increasing her vocabulary (and one who wanted desperately to please her father), Katie would listen intently, however, she was confused with her father's concept of humility. Katie would think, "Why

159

would I ever want to choose to be embarrassed or made fun of? Why would I ever want to be HUMILIATED?"

It was at this tender age that Katie realized it was important to ask more questions. "Humility" sounded so much like **humiliation** that she interrogated her father. He laughed, appreciating Katie's inquisitiveness, and then explained the difference to her. His explanation stuck with her well into adulthood. He warned...

"Humility is not humiliating."

He went on to clarify that if a person doesn't understand the difference, they could fall into the humiliating situation of being humiliatingly UN-HUMBLE. LOL!

As much as we'd like to think that people might **lack humility** due to confusion of the definition or by mistaking it for humiliation, we understand that there is so much more to it than naivety or vocabulary confusion. Often the stereotype of the quintessential salesperson is one of a loud, overconfident and sometimes an arrogant dude. We've all seen what happens when a group of salespeople circle up and engage in a **boastapallooza**. This is that wonder of wonders where they all try to **one-up** each other in a locker room type environment, strutting, peacocking and bragging until their eyes are crossed and the bar is closed down.

Sometimes this type of banter can be misconstrued as swagger, but what does it really **accomplish**? Where is the line between confidence and cockiness, and why does it matter? We believe it matters because too many of us lose sight of that line, and then it limits our growth and the fruit of our efforts.

"Where is the line between confidence and cockiness, and why does that matter?"

It's ironic that, in this day and age, we observe people talking about the importance of, "being humble." The **#humble** hash tag yields millions of posts on Instagram. People use it on posts where they throw up overly filtered selfies and other brags. Other trendy clichés such as **#behumble** can be found under a picture of a perfect looking person wearing expensive Nike Yeezy sneakers. This conspicuous consumption (and other stupid human tricks) demonstrates how we, as a society, so severely mishandle the word humility.

To place a cherry on the top of this hash tag sundae, we'll offer you the final puzzling handle, **#humblebrag**. If this moniker doesn't embody a contradiction in terms, we're not sure what does. All of these social media reflections can teach us something—why it's important to **rise above** all of this craziness and to make a conscious decision to PRACTICE humility and be a bit different than your Gen Y or Z brothers and sisters. Self worth, self love and self-confidence are essential, however, getting (and staying) there without the "brag" can be a slippery slope.

> *"Self worth, self love and self-confidence are essential, however, getting (and staying) there without the 'brag' can be a slippery slope."*

Bottom line, it's NOT all about YOU! We prefer to challenge salespeople to look around and recognize that there are many people that spring from their environment to play a part in their triumphs and are significant reasons for their success.

One of our favorite football coaches of all time, John Madden, said:

> *"Self-praise is for losers. Be a winner. Stand for something. Always have class and be humble."*

One more quote (from Dwayne Johnson) that reinforces this attitude is:

> *"I'm often asked, 'What's the secret to your success?' But there are no secrets. Be humble, be hungry, and always be the hardest worker in the room."*

What does it mean to 'be humble?' Webster's definition of humble is:

The MODEST opinion or estimate of one's own importance

But how does this relate to sales, and how does practicing humility give us strength?

We human beings are flawed. We jump into a sales career and they tell us that we have to **look** and **act** confident to survive and thrive. We're scared to death, so we overcompensate. If we're fortunate enough to have a win or two, we can become prideful—even arrogant. It's in this state of **conceit** where all the bad stuff happens. There are many reasons to exercise the mindset of humility, however below are three of the more important reasons:

The Strengths Humility Provides Us

Increased Professional GROWTH

We can only go **so far** based on our own ideas, paradigms and abilities. There are definite limitations to being shut down, and when we're prideful and arrogant, we are always shut down. If we can flip the script and practice humility, we can **begin to grow again**. We can gain valuable insights through books, mentors, peers and coaches. Humility promotes **receptivity** to all forms of learning. Knowledge equals strength and our results (and income) will increase as a result of staying humble.

COLLABORATION with Peers

Regardless of if we are independent sales professionals (working solo) or if we're in a position of sales leadership, our peers and teammates will be much more inclined to work with us if we are humble and open. The benefits of regularly meeting with and sharing best practices with a group of peers can be amazing. Peers tend to see things in our habits, behaviors and methods that we may never see. (We call these our blind spots) Peer mentorship also offers us another unique benefit. Our peers have no dog in the fight. Often they are brutally honest with us—which is something we need in our lives.

Overcoming OBSTACLES (...and running LEVEL)

Anyone that's been in the game of sales for a while knows that there are **ups** and **downs**, and there are more DOWNS than ups. While this is an unchangeable facet of the game, how we deal with it is strictly our choice. How we handle ourselves in both victory and defeat will determine what our momentum will look like moving forward.

If we are **humble** in our **WINS** we can maintain a healthy perspective without becoming distracted in a place of self-centered grandeur. If we are **humble** and level in our **LOSSES** it will allow us to move past them quickly, and also learn from them. This mindset will allow us to appreciate the struggle for what it gives us as we move toward sustained success.

The practice (and attitude) of humility takes work.

Again, we are not suggesting that you walk around with the burden of self-deprecation or humiliation. This sets you up for failure. Nor are we telling you that you can't have a certain amount of pride—pride is a good thing. We are simply warning you about what ills can happen if you move to a place of arrogance. In our way of thinking, it's all about making a choice each day to practice humility. Doing so will assist you in so many ways inside of your sales career.

Practicing humility is not humiliating. Conversely, it provides you with great strength so that you can build a phenomenal career.

CHAPTER 22

The Voices in Your Head

A 3-step process for self-talk modification

TRACI BATTEN WITH JOE BUZZELLO

*"Words form the thread on which we string our experiences. Therefore, be careful how you interpret your life. Don't think or **speak** negatively lest your subconscious take you at your **word** and you are hung by your own tongue!"*

—ALDOUS HUXLEY

You can't flip on the television or look at your laptop without seeing multiple advertisements for some sort of weight loss product, health related aid or nutritional supplement. Advertisers will tell you over and over again what you SHOULD or should not put into your body. Sure... we want our bodies to function well and look good. But what about our heads? Nobody talks about what the heck we PUT in there!

"...What about our heads?
Nobody talks about what the heck we PUT in there!"

The way we take care of the space between our ears is just as critical as the way we should work on our bodies. The old saying, "An apple a day will keep the doctor away" is fine and still good general advice, but if we apply that prudent suggestion to our bodies only, we miss an important opportunity. We fail to control what we *feed* our minds. We're careless with thoughts that can incubate into negative self-talk. We don't catch faulty verbalizations that eventually become destructive behaviors. In short, we will become, as Aldous Huxley says, "hung by our own tongue."

In this chapter we are going to take a look at what happens if we're not intentional about our thoughts, self-talk and corresponding behavior. Since we are not accredited behavioral psychologists, we are going to tread lightly, but we will take you down an easily understandable pathway—one that will help you recognize how you evolved to where you ARE at right now. In addition to understanding the things that have shaped your self-talk, we'll then offer some tools that may help you jump to a better, more refined place.

Our Scripting

It starts with our parent's voices and the environment in which we were raised. As children, we unconsciously make a set of decisions in response to parental messages about self, others and the world. These decisions are swayed by our **perception** and **interpretation** of what's happening around us. So scripting is more about the interpretation of messages rather than the messages themselves. In addition, a child will do whatever gives them **membership** in the family. We acquire clever survival techniques as a child that actually become limiting in adulthood. We develop self-talk quite early based on our scripting, but as we move into adulthood, we rarely stop to **examine** what parts of our scripting and self-talk can be harmful to us.

"We develop self-talk quite early based on our scripting, but as we move into adulthood, we rarely stop to examine what parts of our scripting and self-talk can be harmful to us."

Traci thinks back about her childhood and she fondly recalls the love that existed. She had a wonderful mother and father. However, she can now identify that there was a very evident **scarcity mindset** in her home. For her it was all very subtle, but she was scripted to **hold onto everything** that she had, for fear of losing it all. So there was definitely a scarcity thing going on and Traci's self-talk took on aspects of controlling and/or hoarding as a result of that scripting.

Much the same was true with Joe and his childhood. He came from a loving, well-meaning, middle-class family that was strictly ruled by a matriarchal depression-era mother. It was common for Joe's mom to say things such as, "Money doesn't make you happy," or, "Rich people are different than us."

It was almost as if Traci and Joe were being **programmed** to be fearful (or even abhorrent) of any success that could come their way. So your life scripting (from an early age) can be huge, and the self-talk that lingers from your earliest years can be quite **limiting**, but there's an equally diminishing factor that evolves during adulthood.

ENVIRONMENTAL CHOICES

We have a tendency to **ignore** a lot of things that creep into our personal environment. These things can include what we **read, listen to, watch**, etc. And then there are our daily habits—the things we do when we first wake up in the morning. From the moment we awake, we're feeding our mind, spirit and attitude. You may want to ask;

- *What does my **morning routine** look like?*
- *How does my **family** support what I'm trying to build?*
- *Which **close friends** represent my external support system?*
- *Are they **supportive** of my dreams and ventures?*

- *Are my friends **positive** people?*
- *Are they **growing** personally and professionally? (As I'm trying to do)*
- *What do they **SAY** to me when I'm struggling?*
- *Do they **reinforce** my progressive thoughts? Or do they tear it down?*

COMBINED EFFECTS

Stop and think about the combined effects of our earliest life scripting (good, bad or indifferent) and all of the digital and human input that flies at our face each day. It's kind of a big deal—and most people DON'T stop to recognize these potentially demoralizing combined effects.

In fact, most people just **exist**...mindlessly, with no real regard or plan to take control of the coding that HAS and IS going on inside of their heads. Worse, we rarely notice how all of this affects our inner-voice and the words that come out of our mouths. Bottom line, we're either getting programmed or we're intentionally **controlling** our own programming.

> *"Bottom line, we are either getting programmed or we're intentionally controlling our own programming."*

Let's discuss what really happens in sales (and our entrepreneurial ventures) as a result of the faulty programing—and what we can do about it.

BECOMING AWAKE (...TO THE VOICES IN OUR HEADS)

We'd like you to become cognizant of the voices in your own head. We know that when we become more aware of what we are thinking—and **WHERE** those thoughts come from—many things can begin to change for the better. In fact, we can learn how to **filter** our thoughts (the voices in our head) and control them before they become words and actions that are destructive to our goals.

Example:

A salesperson wakes up on a Monday morning and thinks:

"I don't know if I want to get out of bed and go to work today. Ugh...it's going to be a hot day and I'm scheduled to go prospecting. I hate cold-calling."

These kinds of thoughts can easily give birth to **feelings** that become **unproductive actions.** Left unchecked, this same salesperson will roll over instead of rolling OUT of bed, eventually telling their spouse, "Honey, I don't feel well, I'm going to grab another hour of sleep." The same person sends a text to their sales manager telling them that they have a "migraine" or some other phantom malady.

Our fictitious salesperson eventually gets out of bed and rolls into the shower, but it's 9:45 am, and by the time they get to the office or out in the field to make a half-hearted attempt to do some prospecting, it may be time for lunch. If ANY prospecting gets done at all, it doesn't happen with a great deal of energy or passion...and their work probably doesn't yield any tangible results.

And the **lost day** all starts with an **unproductive little thought.**

How many of these *lost days* do you need to string together to run yourself right OUT of commission sales?

Hopefully our point is clear. These unhelpful voices in our head that come from faulty life scripting, unsupportive family, negative friends, whatever, MUST be **recognized** and **mitigated.** Become **awake** to the negative self-talk BEFORE it turns into negative emotions that cause words and actions that take you **further away** from your stated goals.

What if you learned how to **quarantine** destructive thoughts and **think** about them? (YES...we're asking you to think about your thoughts!) IF you think about them, you'll immediately recognize those that are harmful to your career. You may even **ERASE** them. You can just as easily **REPLACE** them with thoughts like this:

"This is going to be a great day of prospecting. I GET to get out of bed, shower and go out to share my message. I bet I'll meet a few people that have

*interest in what we do. Those prospects will change
the trajectory of my month. This will be fun."*

If we reframe our self-talk it changes our energy, feelings and actions. If our fictitious salesperson does this, then they'll jump into the shower and they will be making their first sales call by 8:15 am. By lunch, our salesperson will be exhausted, but they will have set three decision-maker meetings! Our salesperson will be feeling pretty good!

So let's break down the **3 steps of modification** so that you can duplicate this method and take dominion over the words and voices that pop into your head.

3-STEP PROCESS FOR SELF-TALK MODIFICATION

Step 1: THINK about your thoughts (monitor and tag)

This sounds weird, but we actually want you to become extremely **conscious** of the words, sentences and alien voices that pop into your head. Simply recognize what sounds:

- Positive
- Neutral
- Negative

If the voices in your head sound positive or neutral, then...no worries. They probably don't require any additional attention. However, if you identify and 'tag' them as **negative** in any way, we'd like you to move to Step 2.

Step 2: Determine the ORIGIN (+ quarantine)

As you catch and 'tag' a thought as negative or destructive to your energy and activities, we'd like you to determine **where** the thought may have emanated from. Ask, "What forces may be triggering these voices in my head?"

You can begin to identify, arrest and quarantine situations that produce negative thoughts, emotions or responses. The practice of learning the root cause of negative thoughts can help you modify your **external sources of input**. You can begin to **move away** from the people or scenarios that are a catalyst for unhelpful thoughts.

Step 3: Erase and Replace (Shift energy)

So far you've taken notice of the thoughts in your head that are not beneficial and tagged them as potentially **damaging** to your objectives. Also, you have done some work to recognize what factors may be **causing** this faulty self-talk so that you can limit that exposure.

Now it's time for you to **erase** and **replace** those destructive words and voices in your head with **positive** and progressive ones.

For example, if the undesirable thought is:

> *"I don't want to do any follow-up work today.*
> *They'll just all say NO or blow me off."*

You'll **erase** that thought and **replace** it with a thought or piece of self-talk that is reasonably positive and honest, and one that **supports** the **work** that you **intend** to do:

> *"I'm going to call back the twenty prospects that are earmarked in my CRM for follow-up today. I have no idea who's going to say YES or NO, and I'm not emotionally connected to either response. It's simply my job to tell my story and identify people that have a need for what I sell. And, oh...I bet that one or two prospects will want to move forward...and that's all I'm really looking for."*

A few obvious **benefits** will ensue as you begin to practice the 3-step process for self-talk modification:

- You will become **quite cognizant** of your own **thoughts**, negative, neutral and positive. And this is a good thing!

- It will begin to become **very evident** to you what factors, forces, input and people cause you to form negative self-talk.
- You will naturally begin to **move away** from harmful forces.
- It will become **second nature** for you to **erase** and **replace** negative thoughts.
- Your **energy** for doing the work will **increase**.
- The **words** coming out of your **mouth** will become more positive and **productive**.
- The actual **results** you have will surely **improve**.

We love this quote by the MMA champion, Rose Namajunas:

"I definitely tend to get down on myself. I needed to work on my self-talk. The same way you do footwork drills and cardio training, I have to do self-talk training."

What we'd like you to walk away from this chapter understanding is, the voices in your head are **powerful**, far more dominant than we often realize. It is our wish for you to start practicing the 3-step process for self-talk modification so that the words that form the thread in your head don't take you further away from your goals.

Again, as the great philosopher, Aldous Huxley tells us:

"...Be careful how you interpret your life. Don't think or speak negatively lest your subconscious take you at your word and you are hung by your own tongue!"

SECTION 6

Focus + Execution

*Creating **CLEAR** paths, staying on the peaks (and out of the valleys) and changing critical **execution** behaviors.*

CHAPTER 23

Just Focus, Dude!

Creating a clear (centering) mindset

CHUCK FARMER WITH JOE BUZZELLO

*"The biggest challenge with staying focused is exercising **discipline** when there are so many other things contending for your head space."*

—JOE BUZZELLO

fo·cus / ˈfōkəs/ *noun*

1. the **center** of interest or activity
2. the state or quality of having or producing **clear** visual **definition**

Don't miss this...
"The **CENTER** of interest or activity."

For sales professionals, the **center** of interest at any one time can be prospecting, following up, closing, fulfilling, servicing etc. If you lead a team, your centers of interest can also include: recruiting, on-boarding, training and coaching. So there's a lot to do and the difficulty we all encounter is focusing long enough on any one or two of those things to achieve concentrated results in those key areas.

If you do a Google search for the phrase, "average attention span," you'll find numerous entries—as you might expect. But what we found most amusing is the fact that the average attention span of a goldfish is about **9 seconds**, and according to a 2015 study from Microsoft Corporation, people lose concentration after only **8 seconds**. In essence, this means if you're a sales trainer, it may be easier for you to train a goldfish than a human being! LOL!

> *"...If you're a sales trainer, it may be easier for you to train a goldfish than a human being!*

The researchers referenced surveyed 2,000 participants and studied the brain activity of 112 others using electroencephalograms. They found that since the year 2000 (or about when the mobile revolution began) the average attention span **dropped** from 12 seconds to 8 seconds. This emphasizes the affects that our increasingly digitized lifestyle has had on our brains. The report also said, "Heavy multi-screeners find it difficult to filter out irrelevant stimuli—they're **more easily distracted** by multiple streams of media."

Microsoft's various surveys also confirmed generational differences for mobile use; for example, 77% of people ages 18–24 responded, "yes" when asked, "When nothing is occupying my attention, the first thing I do is reach for my phone." If we are Gen X or Boomers, our dependence on tech may not be that severe, but can we agree that, regardless of our generation, we often suffer from an inability to focus long enough on a thing to get the results we need? If we factor in times when our thoughts, mood and attitude are negative, it affects our ability to focus even more—it seems impossible to stay on task.

> *"...But can we agree that, regardless of our generation, we often suffer from an inability to focus long enough on a thing to get the results we need?"*

So, when we say something flippant like, "Just focus, dude," we know that it's not easy and there are many emotional, digital and societal disruptions. When Chuck was new to the B2B sales game several decades ago, he recognized that his job was to prospect for long hours at a time. But he often found it hard to maintain focus. He was thinking about all the, "NOs," he had received the day before, or the jerk that was rude to him. And in addition, he often fixated on how badly he needed to create a commissionable opportunity. While we know that these types of behaviors are detrimental (and can be soul sucking) Chuck wasn't even dealing with all of the **digital white noise** that now competes for our headspace.

The digital age hadn't happened yet!

But Chuck knew that he needed to stay very much in the **present**. All killer sales pros understand that you MUST focus on the actions that are most essential to your business. You cannot allow yourself to reflect on what happened in the **past**, or what may, or may not happen in the **future**. In addition, you most certainly can't allow all of the digital white noise to sidetrack you from what is mission-critical to your business. We always (religiously) need to ask, "What actions will positively impact my business today? What should I be focusing on right now?"

> ***"...What actions will positively impact my business today? What should I be focusing on right now?"***

We know...easier said than done. We know how crazy our lives and schedules can be. Whether you began your sales career several decades ago, as Joe and Chuck did, or whether you started yesterday, it's hard to focus. The greatest challenge we'll face in this area is exercising the discipline needed when there are so many other things contending for our headspace.

We're going to dedicate the balance of this chapter to a few simple steps that will help you create a **clear** and **centering** mindset. If you practice the five approaches outlined below, we are quite sure that your mindset surrounding focus will become stronger and better results will follow.

5 Steps to Improved FOCUS

1. Create Clarity (Know what's essential)

It is said that Bill Belichick, coach of the New England Patriots, stalks the sidelines on a Sunday, asking his players, "Do you know your job?" That's a great question, but DO you **know** your job? Are you **100% clear** on **what moves your needle**? Is your day/week then scheduled (planned) to produce maximum results in your immediate areas of focus? The answers to these questions force a great kind of clarity.

2. Run an Air-Tight Schedule (Hardwire the time)

We've often said, "If it's not IN your calendar **it doesn't exist**." The people that kill it in sales and entrepreneurial ventures *commit* (hard wire) blocks of FOCUSED time in their calendars in order to accomplish the things that will absolutely move their business forward. They don't leave anything to chance. The calendars are very **intentional**.

3. Eliminate Distractions (During your prime-time)

Stone cold sales pros all know what their prime selling time is and they *guard* that time fiercely. They don't clown around and they don't let any external clowns get in their way. Bottom line, they **calculatedly eliminate all interruptions**. This includes personal stuff. They train their loved ones that their "work time" must be used for productive and disciplined activities—just as if they were on the clock at an office. It's not that they ignore their family; it's just that **they create professional boundaries**. They don't succumb to time vampires or stupid human tricks at the office. They go into the office, get what they need and then they get their rear ends back into the field. They also control all digital white noise.

4. Create Quiet Time (Planned breaks)

We've found very few people that can run (with their blinders on) and do a decent job at a task for more than 2 – 4 hours at a time. Make sure you **come up for air** once in a while during your day. Short breaks and a relaxing lunch can do wonders for your daylong attentional energy. This is the time to get on social media, your favorite sports app, make personal calls, rewind, etc.

5. *Know Your Body (Diet + energy)*

FUEL your body properly. It's so easy to pull into a fast food restaurant and fill up quickly and cheaply. BUT your body will respond negatively to that type of fuel. You put **premium gas** in a high performing car, and you should treat your body the same way.

Be sure to drink plenty of water. Coffee is a great drink to start your day, but avoid the high sugar, highly caffeinated energy drinks. Chuck loves to drink a Coke as much as anyone, but we all know these types of beverages have no redeeming qualities long term.

In addition, avoid foods high in saturated fats and eat clean meats and vegetables. Chuck used to love a good Pizza Hut buffet for lunch, however, as you can imagine, his afternoon wasn't very focused or effective after a chowing down like that. It's easy to stop at a fast food restaurant and eat a quick, tasty, cheap meal. It takes more effort and **discipline** to make better choices that will allow us to focus on our mission. The good news is that there are more and more restaurants that cater to a healthy lifestyle, and even the fast food chains offer more healthy choices than ever before.

So these five steps are simple in nature and we believe that, if practiced, they can change your ability to create clarity and stay focused. But while these are straightforward steps, they may not be easy for you to adopt and adapt to if your current habits in these areas greatly differ. In that case, you will have to summon great discipline. We know this because we have coached many salepeople and we understand that, in today's world, there are a lot of things competing for mind space.

You must make a decision that you are going to **modify a few behaviors** and attitudes in this area. But once you do, you will be able to focus and center yourself, create far better results than you had before, and your business will be more fun.

Let's get clear and centered on the job at hand.

Let's get focused, dude!

CHAPTER 24

Peaks + Valleys

Not getting STUCK in between

DAWN TYACK WITH JOE BUZZELLO

*"Do the difficult things while they are **easy**, and do the great things while they are **small**."*

—LAO TZU

It's so hard to watch.

But sometimes that's all you can do.

He put in a lot of hard work. He did what we asked him to do—made prospecting a priority and diligently worked the system we layed out for him. He had his first small victory in no time flat. He connected with the right person, set the appointment, scheduled a presentation and it closed.

Awesome!

Then it happened.

Over the next several weeks he became almost exclusively focused on his enticing (upcoming) sale. He **obsessed** on it to the exclusion of everything else. He persuaded himself that the **singular** opportunity must be his priority. He convinced himself that he didn't have the time to continue filling his pipeline or working the system that had begun to WORK for him. He *neglected* the activities that brought him his initial win in the first place.

We know you get this—he wanted to *feel* the rush of achievement—bask in the glow of it. He told himself, "I'll prospect later, when I have a little more time." He was savoring today's victory, but also setting the stage for tomorrow's defeat. He was allowing himself to slip right off of a peak into a deep dark valley.

> **"He was savoring today's victory, but also
> setting the stage for tomorrow's defeat."**

This is what we want you to understand, **between** the victorious peaks of a sale (or multiple sales), lay **treacherous valleys**. These valleys are strewn with the bones of the salespeople who failed to build suspension bridges—the ones necessary to traverse from peak to peak. It happens slowly at first. The signs of slippage can be almost undetectable. It starts with **small excuses**—ones you don't even realize you're making. It can be subtle stuff—the narrative doesn't sound as obvious as, "I'm going to take the day off because I deserve it, #treatmyself." It sounds more like, "I'm too busy to focus on anything but this sale." Again...hard to detect...the devil doesn't show up in a red suit with a pitch fork.

Bottom line, when you *neglect* any of the the foundational systems (or work) that make a sale possible in the first place, it will be the **downfall** of your month, quarter, year or even your career—you'll slip off the peak into the valley below.

> **"...When you neglect any of the the foundational
> systems (or work) that make a sale possible in
> the first place, it will be the downfall of your
> month, quarter, year or even your career."**

So, a few questions that we'll ask in this chapter:

- What does it look like when you move from **PEAK** to **PEAK**?
- Is it possible to **avoid VALLEYS** completely?
- When you wind up in a **VALLEY**, how do you mitigate it—not get **STUCK** down there?

PEAK TO PEAK MINDSET

This attitude requires highly disciplined thinking and actions. It's hard. We're not going to kid you, this is one of those philosophies that only killers—the top 20 %—adopt and practice. It requires a person to set many of their typical emotions on a shelf. It requires complete **dedication** and **accountability** to certain thoughts, disciplines and actions. There can't be an ounce of laziness if you're going to consistently go from peak to peak and not visit any of the ever-present valleys.

Here are a few of the elements that comprise this mindset. We'll attempt to break them down for you:

Build Mental Suspension Bridges:

This mental hack requires that you think in terms of building suspension bridges between peaks by **ALWAYS prospecting** while you are managing your whirlwind of duties. In other words, you take care of business, but never at the *expense* of prospecting. You're always prospecting at the **same time** you're attending to the other important and/or urgent stuff.

The moment you **abandon** prospecting disciplines, you begin the downward slide into the pit of the valley. Your trajectory shifts down, you lose momentum. Get ready for a **long, dry walk** down in that valley before you are able to get pointed uphill again. So this element is simply a mental commitment to never shut down your prospecting machine—not even for a moment. This ensures that you will have a smooth traverse between peaks.

We opened this chapter with a quote from the ancient Chinese philosopher, Lao Tzu.

> *"Do the difficult things while they are easy, and do the great things while they are small."*

The great philosopher's words totally **apply** to us sales folk.

In application, this means that it's a lot **easier** to prospect and **add** future opportunities to your pipeline when you are up there on a peak—riding a wave of positive momentum. When you're down in the darkness of the valley it's significantly harder. Just think about how difficult it is to get your process started all over again from a **cold start**, when you haven't had a win in a while and **your pockets are empty**. We want you to build your bridges as you move along—when it's easiest—when you're on top of the world with a big smile on your face. You **POUR it on!** This is what the killer pros do!

> *"We want you to build your bridges as you move along—when it's easiest—when you're on top of the world with a big smile on your face."*

Practice Intentional Calendaring: (Hardwiring)

This is a very straightforward **practice** that begins with a consistent and disciplined mindset and then transforms into an incredibly important **calendar habit**. The disciplined mindset part of this is when a salesperson learns that there is rarely (if ever) a priority that rises above prospecting. This practice continues with the habit of intentionally calendaring **blocks of time** that are only to be used for focused and high quality prospecting work.

We call this, "**hardwiring**." The best of the best simply force prospecting time into their calendar up front—before the week begins—and they don't violate those precious blocks of time. They are sacrosanct. When this type of mindset and calendar discipline match up, it becomes very powerful. A salesperson has begun to build a marketing machine for themselves, one that will not fail them.

Monitor the Voices In Your Head:

We can't ignore the voices in our head—the ones that keep us up at night. A **Peak-to-Peak** mindset requires that you consistently fight the toughest foe we all have. It's US. Specifically, our inner dialogue! We must rewire that faulty stuff. If we are going to win we have to condition ourselves to recognize BS excuses. With this element we get to flick the little devil off our shoulder—get him out of our ear! Only then will we be able to move from peak-to-peak, traversing along the suspension bridges of our sales system.

Recognizing A Valley (The obvious)

It's a real world.

In all of our combined years of sales training and management, we've never seen a salesperson so perfect in their mindsets, skillsets, calendar disciplines that they didn't blink and lose momentum. In addition to all of the forced errors, there are **unforced** ones. Stuff happens in life that knocks us off our peak and down into that valley. I'm referring to personal issues, kids, illness, emergencies, etc. So it's going to happen...even if you're a killer, eventually, you'll find yourself in a valley. So let's deal with that— let's look at what happens with these valleys and what's important for you to think about.

Reality Check:

Job ONE is for you to open your eyes and **DETERMINE** where you're really **at** in any given period of time. Don't operate in fantasy land, instead diagnose your current position. If you're in a **SLUMP**, then recognize it— admit that fact to yourself and your mentors. Give it a name if you have to, but for the love of God...**don't ignore it!** It's not like it's going to go away if you pretend it's not there.

Be a master of the obvious realities.

Decision Time:

Then, at once—right when you identify that you are slipping into a valley—**STOP**. Create ten minutes of space and make a concious decision. Make the decision that you will do **whatever it takes** to stop the plunge and build your bridge back to the next peak.

That's it.

Just do those two things.

ASCENDING OUT OF THE VALLEY (GETTING UN-STUCK)

Okay, congratulations. You've realized that you've slid either partially or wholly down the mountainside into a valley. In addition, you've made a decision to get off your rusty dusty butt and do what it takes to ascend to that next peak. So what are the steps that the killers take when this happens to them?

The Mental RESET Button:

We're going to ask you to hit your mental **reset button**. This is a very straightforward practice that all winners use when they get a bit off track. What they do is simply hit the *erase* button in their head—they immediately **STOP** thinking and doing anything (and everything) that's unproductive.

They wipe their **mental chalkboard** clean.

Back to SYSTEM Basics:

We all have a number of things that have always worked for us. The best of the best simply go back to those things—they begin to WORK what has always WORKED for them. While it starts with erasing a flawed mental chalkboard, it continues with their resolution to *resume* the **proven** prospecting and selling systems. It then extends to their calendar disciplines.

It almost sounds too cliché, but the real pros go **back to basics** when they notice they are slumping.

"We all have a number of things that have always worked for us. The best of the best simply go back to those things—they begin to WORK what has always WORKED for them."

So there you have it.

Peaks are great, but valleys DO exist.

If you spend most of your time on a peak, you are doing all of the right things. When you find yourself in a valley, **you now know** what the pros do (mentally and practically) to get themselves out of those valleys. Great salespeople and entrepreneurs choose to learn from the lessons that the valley teaches. **They reflect** on the counterproductive narrative and unproductive practices that they'd been lazily indulging in.

"Great salespeople and entrepreneurs choose to learn from the lessons that the valley teaches."

Simply stated, they snap out of it and **BEGIN** again.

They start building suspension bridges as soon as they realize their position. A Peak-to-Peak mindset fosters a work atmosphere that favors stability. It requires attitudes that establish conditions for consistent success. It curbs the fear, dread, and anxiety that may follow long bouts of low production.

Set your **MIND** and your eyes on the next peak. Don't stop prospecting and building bridges just because you've had some low level or moderate forms of success. That kind of mindset has never worked and it never will.

Those who build wealth in the game of sales don't get stuck in the valleys.

CHAPTER 25

Execution Codes

A mindset that changes critical behaviors

EMILY EVANS WITH JOE BUZZELLO

*"But, in fact, **discipline** is the pathway to freedom."*
—JOCKO WILLINK

Alex (not his real name) was a skilled salesperson that had become a new sales manager. Joe had appointed him to a leadership role and watched him grow...and then he noticed that Alex had stopped growing. As Joe dug in, it became clear that Alex was having a hard time executing on a few of the more critical aspects of his job.

When Alex was just a salesperson, he executed well and his production was quite good. In his third year, he was offered the opportunity to build a sales team. At first, he maintained solid personal production as he began to field train a few of the new salespeople that were assigned to him. However, as his team grew and his overall responsibilities expanded, he became **paralyzed** in certain areas. Critical aspects of his business were being partially or wholly **ignored**. His personal production also began to fade.

When Joe finally reached down several levels to try to correct Alex's situational path, it was almost too late. Alex's first comment to Joe was, "I just wish I was a producer again. This all feels overwhelming to me...I can't seem to get anything done—my desk is covered with crap. I know I'm blowing it big time."

As Joe talked him "off the ledge", LOL...he began to clarify what Alex's biggest pain points were...and they all revolved around **execution**—or the lack of it—in one way or another.

If you think about it, we all have areas in our professional and personal lives where we are deadly good at getting things done. Conversely, we all have areas where we become partially or completely **jammed up**—where we can't seem to execute. These executable items can be simple things, like being on time to a meeting, or preparing a meal. They can also be tougher items like completing a task that you have some degree of **fear** attached to—such as cold calling—or giving a presentation to a key prospect. We can stall or get stuck easily when we are asked to execute on a task that we have **never completed before** or one where we feel out of our element—one that is outside of our core competency. Lastly, we can become completely bound and gagged when the thing we're trying to execute on seems **too big** to us—or even unimaginable to attain.

> ### *"...We can become completely bound and gagged when the thing we're trying to execute on seems too big to us—or even unimaginable to attain."*

So there Alex was...suffering from most of those execution-killing ailments! He was lost and losing, and his attitude about things sucked. He went from being an effective and profitable sales producer to a struggling failing sales manager. As Joe sat with Alex that day, he noticed that he was very honest and transparent. The **words** and **phrases** he used to describe what was going on in his head, on his desk and in his calendar sounded like this:

> *Fear – completely unfamiliar – crushing – feels awkward – distractions – very uncomfortable – paralyzed – no confidence – too much – too big*

Alex was trippin' for sure, but his case isn't unique and a great coach can help a willing student, and he happened to be sitting across the table from a couple of great sales coaches. ☺

We all get into this business of commission sales in the hope and faith that we will become financially free at some juncture. We learn how to survive, and then we may even begin to thrive. Then one day we wake up and we realize we have stopped growing. Many of the words and phrases that Alex spewed forth (above) may then come into play, and then:

- *We start to feel overwhelmed*
- *Our disciplines slowly break down*
- *Structure collapses*
- *Behavior deteriorates*
- *We begin to shut down*
- *And then, we **stop executing** on critical initiatives*

ESTABLISHING YOUR EXECUTION CODES *(RULES)*

So think about a task like washing the dishes. Emily will tell you that she has an extreme dislike for doing dishes. Emily used to wait until the dishes were piled high—the sink was full and the plates, cups and silverware were overflowing onto the counter.

Some of you are asking...

> ### *"Okay, Emily, how could you let that mess get so big?"*

Good and fair question, but we're not going to send Emily to a therapist to find out. Maybe she feared hot water and dish soap? Maybe she thought that she wasn't good at washing dishes. Perhaps she got distracted with the family just after dinnertime. But **does it really matter** what the reason was? The bottom line was...the dishes were piling up and it was a mess! She'd let it get way out of hand—it had become a monstrous task— one that was going to take WAY too much time!

EMILY ESTABLISHED A CODE

What if Emily applied one small **mindset hack** to this scenario? What if she simply created a **code** (or rule) for herself and the family? And what if that code or rule **changed her behavior?**

Emily made a small mindset change. The voice in her head told her, "Hey, if you do the dishes after each meal, rather than waiting, the dishes don't actually take that long to do, and your kitchen will always be presentable...and you'll feel better." As a result of Emily establishing this **rule**, her behavior (and the family's conduct) changed. Her new code—the one she decided to live by—was that the dishes would be quickly and efficiently washed, put away (or placed in the dishwasher) **immediately after** each meal, every evening, before Netflix is turned on.

No fail.

CHANGING CRITICAL BEHAVIORS

What happened in Emily's kitchen after that? Simply put, Emily identified an area that she was not executing well on, then she trained herself to obey a code of behavior that empowered her to **complete a task** without a great deal of **emotion** or feelings involved.

> *"...She trained herself to obey a code of behavior that empowered her to complete a task without a great deal of emotion or feelings involved."*

If you're tracking with us, then you've figured out that it revolves around one simple but powerful word:

DISCIPLINE

If you closely examine what stone-cold sales and sales management pros do (regarding) execution, it looks a lot like this word, discipline. **Discipline** and **self-controls** are a HUGE part of getting things done.

Let's examine how you can **apply** this mindset to every critical task or initiative that you **must execute** on. We will walk you through four simple steps that will help you establish and follow your codes and rules.

4 STEPS TO EXECUTION

1. *IDENTIFY The Critical Tasks (That you must execute on)*

Ask, "What are the one, two or three **most important** strategies, tasks or activities that I will need to execute on in order to move my needle?" Be mindful that there probably aren't dozens of these **important** things to execute on...there are just a few.

2. *CHUNK Those Activities Down (Into something bite size)*

Just like Emily's dishes, if you do a little bit of work on a task each day, it never becomes a big deal and it gets done. Break down (chunk down) these initiatives to monthly, weekly and daily measures. Make these tasks **small** and **clear.**

3. *Create Your CODES (Rules for each critical action)*

As you identify and break down the task/action/activity, then it's time to establish your code or **rules** for it.

For example:

"I prospect on Monday, Wednesday and Thursday during the hours of 8:00 AM to Noon. I reach out to a minimum of _____ prospects during these sessions."

4. *FOLLOW Your Rules Without Fail (Remove emotion)*

This step is where rubber meets the road. This is where you apply discipline to the equation. You will simply **lock into** the rules you've established, removing emotion. You simply follow your code of behavior, regardless of how you *feel*. If you train yourself to practice this code for a few weeks, it will be a behavior that becomes part of your DNA.

Okay, I know you get this. Like most stuff we teach, it's simple—like doing the dishes.

But what about Alex?

Joe was able to walk him through these steps. Joe learned that he was allowing feelings and emotions (and fear) to hijack his daily and weekly routine. Joe and another middle manager were able to help him recognize that there were **just a couple of major objectives** that he'd need to pay close attention to. They showed him how to measure those things in **small weekly chunks**. It then became obvious to Alex that he'd need to hardwire those actions into his calendar. He began to create **his own weekly rules** for those tasks.

And his behavior changed.

And he began to **GROW** again.

Alex actually learned how to create **a code of behavior** for himself. This is also known as **being able to coach yourself** when nobody else is around. And this is a critical tool if you are going to become financially free.

We'll close this chapter with a question. As you look at where you are at in your professional development today, what **Execution Codes** do you need to establish for yourself? What rules (if created and followed with discipline), will begin to change critical behaviors inside of your business?

> *"...What Execution Codes do you need to establish for yourself? What rules (if created and followed with discipline), will begin to change critical behaviors inside of your business?"*

This is a simple mindset hack that will pay **big dividends** to you on your path to financial freedom!

SECTION 7

Time

*Treating time as a **TANGIBLE** commodity, uncapping our time potential, establishing time **primacies** + recognizing our **VALUABLE** sands of time*

CHAPTER 26

Time As a
Tangible Commodity

...versus an elusive idea

BRANDEE JUSTUS WITH JOE BUZZELLO

*"It's impossible to 'manage' time. The best you can do is to
manage YOURSELF **inside of** blocks of time."*

—JOE BUZZELLO

The idea that you can have the freedom to control your own time is one of the most alluring attractions for people entering an independent sales gig.

Ironically, it's also the **greatest cause of failure**.

Most new salespeople don't realize that the freedom to use your time as you wish is a double-edged sword. We are somewhat programmed that

197

if we arrive on time to our jobs at 8:00 am sharp each morning, and if we take an hour for lunch and then leave at 5:00 pm, that makes us good stewards of our time. In reality, if we do exactly that, it only proves that most of us are smart enough not to get fired. However, when a person is placed suddenly in a position where they are given complete freedom to control their time in any way they see fit, they must quickly become DILIGENT **guardians** of their time—or they'll crash and burn.

In our long careers, we have seen and experimented with dozens of time management strategies. What we're repeatedly reminded of is that the key to utilizing your time wisely is to see it as a **tangible commodity** versus just an **elusive idea**.

> ### *"...the key to utilizing your time wisely is to see it as a tangible commodity versus just an elusive idea."*

We all have the same fifty-two weeks each year, seven days each week and twenty-four hours in a day. So why is it that some salespeople and entrepreneurs accomplish three or four times more than others? We believe it boils down to knowing what's vitally important, eliminating what is **not**, and understanding what a **block of time** actually represents for us.

At one juncture, earlier in her career, Brandee was feeling stretched thin. She was leading a team of over fifty salespeople, and had two wonderfully active teenagers at home. She was also trying to carve out some time for herself. Brandee decided to take an eight-week span of time and plan out every minute of her day, starting at 4:30 am and ending at 10:00 pm. Brandee included her drive time to and from every destination. She carefully scheduled and recorded every activity—taking a shower, eating a meal, each meeting, sending emails, verbal communication, time with family—absolutely everything.

Her **deliberate** exercise proved to her that she had significantly more time than she previously realized. Brandee told one good friend that she, "Didn't realize what a 'slacker' she had become." Once those small blocks of time became a **tangible commodity** to her, she began to accomplish so much in a day that it utterly amazed her—it seemed unreal—she was far more productive than she'd ever been.

However, Brandee could only run at that highly organized pace for eight weeks. The reason she couldn't go beyond that span of time was that the planning, scheduling and recording of every single moment became absolutely exhausting to her. During that eight weeks, Brandee had denied herself of any significant down time. Every minute had an objective.

She was burnt!

Many of us have run like this before for short periods of time, and we don't believe that it's something humans can do for long. However, we have learned a great deal from experimental sprints like this. Here are three KEY points we'd like to share on this theme:

1. There is nothing that we don't have time for—only things we're unwilling to *make* time for.
2. Just because something is not considered **productive** doesn't mean that it isn't **time well spent**.
3. **We** can **allow** our calendar to run **us**, or we can **choose** to **run IT**.

Every person we know that has done a **personal time study** has experienced a few surprises.

They're astonished at how much time they actually have. Think about all of the time suckers in your day. Do you arrive so early to meetings that you're sitting fifteen minutes, waiting for them to start? If that occurs once each day, that amounts to an hour or more each week that you're sitting... doing nothing. What about web surfing? Do you scan your personal inbox only to realize (an hour later) that you've planned your fantasy vacation? Do you spend ten minutes every day perusing your closet for the perfect outfit? All of these seemingly **insignificant activities** can really **add up**. The time you actually have available to you is astounding.

The common response, "I don't have time," is simply untrue. Acknowledging this is the first step to understanding that there's always time for what you **choose** to make time for. Have you ever known a salesperson that never had time to prospect, yet always had time to play golf? They convince themselves that their time on the golf course is building their pipeline. They suggest they'll meet three new people in the four hours that they are on the golf course. In reality, those four hours could have been spent making fifty approaches to new, qualified leads. It's the same way for someone that says they never have time to exercise; yet they spend endless hours online researching fad diets and watching cat videos. Bottom line, when something is truly important to you—an absolute priority—you'll find time for it.

> ### "...When something is truly important to you— an absolute priority—you'll find time for it."

Once you realize how much time you actually have, it is imperative that you begin to **OWN** that time, not just for what you *need* to be doing, but also for what you *want* to be doing.

Using that extra time for things that truly make you feel happy (not just accomplished) is **not wasted time**. This is where the work-life balance thing comes into play. It takes time to learn this. Having a thriving career is a huge gift.

So is having a family that you love!

> ### "Having a thriving career is a huge gift. So is having a family that you love."

Like so many self-employed people, Brandee used to carry around a tremendous weight called, "guilt."

And it was a **two-way** guilt.

When she was consumed with work, she'd worry about what was happening at home. When she was entirely immersed in the family, she would feel she should be working to provide more for them. It never even crossed her mind that there could be time just for herself—time that would, ironically, make her **better** in both of those roles. Only when she made a conscious decision to purposefully allocate her time did she realize that there truly was enough time for everything that was important to her. When you're clear on how much time you actually have, and you designate time for personal things you enjoy, as well as your professional objectives, guilt dissolves.

> *"When you're clear on how much time you actually have, and you designate time for personal things you enjoy, as well as your professional objectives, guilt dissolves."*

When it feels like your calendar is running you as opposed to you running your calendar, the chaos is undeniable. The core of the chaos comes from confusing those tasks that seem **urgent** with what is actually **important**.

Have you ever stopped to ask yourself what would happen if you simply didn't take on the responsibility of putting out someone else's fires? It could be the client that doesn't pay their bill on time, but is always shocked when their services are on the verge of suspension. Or maybe it's the teammate that doesn't attend meetings, but doesn't have key information for her job.

> *"Have you ever stopped to ask yourself what would happen if you simply didn't take on the responsibility of putting out someone else's fires?"*

For leaders of large teams, being available to a bunch of people and experiencing interruptions are a significant part of our day. We've often found ourselves working well into the evening to make up the time we'd lost throughout the day. Brandee actually instituted a **rule** for herself. If there was an "emergency" question that she knew could be answered by others, she would wait an hour before responding. She'd text: "I just got a break. Do you still need help?"

What Brandee found was interesting.

When the salespeople who relied on her constantly for **immediate** assistance didn't get immediate answers, they suddenly became resourceful. In today's world of technology and instant communication, we have become conditioned that everything (no matter how minute), needs immediate attention. This way of thinking actually costs us time. There are many things that can be initially *ignored*. While disregarding communication can be considered rude, delaying a response on issues that really aren't urgent is actually very practical.

Consider this. Some people **create fires** only to resent being their own rescue worker later. We all know these people—they shortcut even the most basic tasks, convinced that it won't catch up to them but when it does it's ugly!

An example:

Rick and Molly have a huge collection of ornaments for their Christmas tree. Decorating the tree each year is nothing short of an event. Packing up all of these special ornaments and placing them back into storage each year is a time consuming task. A few years ago, Rick was a bit tired—not into it. With Molly off, traveling for work, the job was left to Rick. Rather than scout out the "right" packaging for each piece, he hastily shoved them all into boxes, paying little attention to the task. It worked great. He saved about two hours on the task.

As Rick and Molly unpacked the ornaments the following season, they found many of them damaged. They were devastated. They wound up spending many hours online over the ensuing weeks searching for duplicates of their most treasured pieces. They also spent hundreds of dollars replacing ornaments that they considered collectors' items. Rick was furious, never acknowledging that he had created the situation in the first place. Molly wondered how Rick could have been so careless. However, Rick is someone known to spend a dollar to save a dime. This example/behavior is also observed in the way some people use their time. Often, procrastinators create the same type of scenarios.

Procrastinators put off their **least favorite** tasks, allowing them to compound until they're close to a full-on disaster if not addressed. Think of the person who isn't feeling great and notices a nodule in their neck but refuses to visit the doctor because they 'don't have time.' Months go by and they're feeling worse. Finally, when they can't stand it any longer, they go to the doctor. They learn they've developed a form of cancer that has progressed. Most of the time procrastinating doesn't create life-threatening situations, but it does create scenarios that can become much more complex (and consuming) to resolve than the original tasks.

Controlling one's own time is not only a **privilege**; it's also a massive **responsibility**. The key to guiding your time effectively is the understanding of this very paradigm. When we begin to think of time as a **tangible commodity**, versus an **elusive idea,** you are developing an extremely valuable attitude. The best we hope to do is to manage OURSELVES inside of small blocks of time, and when we do this intentionally, we can find the powerful balance that most of us seek.

CHAPTER 27

Influencing Your Time

Our untapped superpower

DAWN TYACK WITH JOE BUZZELLO

*"Time = Life, therefore; Waste your time and waste your
life, or **master** your time and master your life."*

—ALAN LAKEIN

We're all very busy people, operating in an unbelievably **noisy** world. Simply think about how technology has changed things over the last few decades, especially for Boomers and the Gen X gang. We've gone from being available during normal work hours on a land line, to being available 24/7 through a myriad of technology platforms including mobile calls, texts, emails, FaceTime, Zoom calls, LinkedIn, Facebook Messenger and our own social walls.

Technology has given your hierarchy, partners, clients and peers the idea that they can **access** you anytime a question, need, directive or cat video crosses their mindspace. And most of these folks have the unrealistic expectation that you are responsible for responding immediately.

You get **hit on** and **pulled on** from every direction.

Your days **blur**—one turns into another, destroying your to-do list and eviscerating your careful plans. All of this leaves critical tasks and actions undone. We start to feel overburdened by how **busy** we feel. Our calendars and schedules become cluttered. We race around trying to keep all of our plates spinning in the air. We fall into the **habit of distraction** easily, and then we jump from task to task, or worse, we attempt to multi-task. And when we do that, our work is completed in a half-assed manner, forcing us to do some of it over. It actually takes us twice as long to get some things done right.

We know we are capable of so much more, hence we ultimately beat ourselves up inside. We fall into the trap of thinking that we simply need more time—we don't have enough time to get everything done—but where do we find this elusive additional time? If only we could go to the local store and buy some **time seeds**. We could then grow a "time garden" and harvest more time.

Okay, put down the edibles.

This isn't the answer. LOL!

If we agree that we can't magically create more time, then can we agree that the answer lies in our mindsets, actions and habits? We'll have to create attitudes and philosophies that help us harness more **control, shape** and **form** over our critically important productive time and family time.

Harnessing this control, shape and form is a resource that each of us has inside of us. It is our latent superpower—we simply need to *activate* it by becoming an **influencer** of time.

Becoming an Influencer of Your Time

In moving to activate this "superpower" inside of you, we'd like you to consider these **mindset-related** steps that can be easily translated into actions:

- Make a pact with yourself that you will regularly (at least weekly) block out the **space** to take a careful (30,000 foot) look at your daily activities.
- Build a **sensitivity** that enables you to proactively **identify** high-priority—high-yield tasks—those things that have the **most impact** on your production and results.
- Create the behavior of intentionally **scheduling** those **actions** and **activities FIRST** in your daily calendar.
- Become painfully honest with yourself. **Identify distractions**, time wasters, and **LOW priority** tasks.
- Create a firm philosophy that allows you to **let go** of these things. *(Eliminate them completely, delegate them, or schedule them during low productivity times)*

Establishing these attitudes and behaviors puts you in a position to win. This **superpower** (influencing your time) is rooted in the concept of becoming **intentional** with respect to how you use your time.

Here are three more key **behavioral mindsets** that we believe are critical in the development of your superpowers over time:

- Concentrate on **ONE** activity at a time. Be **present** for it.
- **Focus** all of your mental and physical resources on the accomplishment of the specific task in front of you.
- Set a **specific amount of time** for the task at hand. Establish **deadlines** for everything.

We gravitate towards procrastinating when we feel overwhelmed. We have learned that procrastination is both a coping mechanism and also a **mindset**, albeit not a very productive or positive one. Taking control of our daily schedule in specific **chunks of time** will help us to clear away the **fog** and direct us down a path of priority—making certain that we do the important things **first**.

> ## *"We gravitate towards procrastinating when we feel overwhelmed."*

Once you have your calendar and work schedule set in stone, then you must remain **faithful** to it and **protective** of it. You must guard against anyone or anything (including yourself) that can *infringe* upon it. Of course, these mindsets **extend beyond** our professional worlds and into our **personal** lives. Consider adopting the following two behaviors:

- **UNPLUG**—turn off your mobile device and all social media when you are with your family or loved ones. Learn to be **unavailable** and be comfortable with that feeling.
- Schedule time to **do nothing.** Become okay with not being productive 24/7. Perhaps this is the time you read a book, put on headphones and listen to your favorite music, or watch an old movie that makes you smile.

In order to rest, rejuvenate and recharge, you will need to create time and space for **yourself.** Scheduling a full day, just for yourself, would be great, but if you can't do that, then at least hardwire some quiet time—perhaps a four hour block of time—to reconnect to what's really important to you.

> ### *"In order to rest, rejuvenate and recharge, you will need to create time and space for yourself."*

As you begin to adopt and practice some of the attitudes, mindsets and behaviors that we have outlined for you in this chapter, you will be surprised at just how **empowered** you start to feel when you engage in the practice of *influencing* your time. By establishing these attitudes and *adhering* to a more intentional calendar, you'll not only get a heck of a lot more done professionally, you will also be able to identify more time for yourself, your family and for living life to the fullest.

These mindsets (and the actions they will promote) will trigger feelings of accomplishment at the end of each day. This will, of course, foster a positive attitude and set you on an **upward spiral.** You'll find that you will systematically begin to achieve your short-term goals, and then, the fulfillment of your long-term goals will become more probable. As you begin to feel more accomplished, a larger world of possibilities will open up.

> *"These mindsets (and the actions they will promote) will trigger feelings of accomplishment at the end of each day. This will, of course, foster a positive attitude and set you on an upward spiral."*

Time is yours to **spend**, just like money; pennies make dollars and seconds make hours. The message here is that you can achieve big goals, gain control of your career (and your life) by simply applying the mindset that it's possible for you to **intentionally influence** your time consistently, each and every day.

We've just uncorked your new superpower.

Grab a cape (and your calendar) and fly with it.

CHAPTER 28

Foundations of Time

Establishing your time primacies

TRACI BATTEN WITH JOE BUZZELLO

*"Either **you** run the day, or the day runs you."*
—JIM ROHN

We try so darn hard to regulate and control our time. Sometimes we try to manage our time so precisely that we reach the point of temporary insanity. Then we give up and go to the **opposite** end of the spectrum—no time boundaries at all.

In this chapter we'll show you how to develop a mindset about TIME that will set you apart from the pack. It's about establishing an underlying **foundational** model of **HOW** and **WHY** you utilize your precious time. If we can get you to develop this foundation, you'll then truly begin to become what you've dreamed of.

211

For many years, Traci's mantra has been:

> ### "If it's dead, dying or on fire, let me know...
> ### and then I might change my schedule."

This may sound hard-core, but Traci established this unique time survival policy because she's the mother of six kids. If you boil down Traci's mantra, it's all about identifying what's urgent and what needs to wait. If you have any kind of a herd at home, like hers, then you know that their needs can pull you in multiple directions at one time, if you allow it. If you couple this parenting thing with the task of starting (or scaling) a business, the STRESS that occurs (when you DON'T create clear **primacies** of time) can kill your career fast. You simply won't last that long in the commission sales game.

> ### "...The STRESS that occurs (when you DON'T create
> ### clear primacies of time) can kill your career fast."

So when Traci was near the end of her rope—close to walking away and admitting defeat in sales—she simply sat down and asked herself TWO key questions, and they sounded something like this:

1. What's most IMPORTANT to me in my life?

Big question, we know! But this is where you start.

For us it's about our spiritual life first, our belief that there is a God above and we're on this earth for a short time. We're also here for a **definite purpose**. Beyond our spiritual beliefs, our thinking then gravitates towards our wonderful families and our closest friends. If you're patriotic, service to your country and community may come next.

You've probably noticed that we've mentioned, God, family, relationships, our country and community...and we haven't gotten to our careers and business yet! That's because of the **vertical alignment** mindset we apply to our use of time. We choose to rank the very most important things first. It's not that our work or careers aren't important; it's just that our professional work has its definite and **intentional place** of importance.

When you establish YOUR vertical alignment, you can begin to take deep breaths and then build out a schedule that acknowledges that everything has its **proper place** in your calendar and deserves its attention in the right amounts and at the appropriate time.

We suggest that you take these logical and intentional steps:

- Reserve time for your **spiritual life**. For most, this will be Sunday and possibly one other weekday evening.
- Then, place all of your **family commitments**, functions, vacations and other important dates in the calendar. You should include your kid's days off from school, long weekends, etc.
- The next thing you're going to have to decide is what time your **storefront opens** each day. There are days when this time might be pushed back if you have a kid's function in the morning, or if you need to assist an aging loved one or something such as this. However, generally, your business day may begin at 8:00 am, which means that all of your personal items are completed **before** 8:00 am.
- You'll learn to adjust your wake-up time to accommodate what's important to you. You can read, write, work out, make breakfast, etc., before you begin to work. **Take care of YOU first** and then begin your professional day.
- You then must decide when your **storefront** should **close** each day, and this is where a lot of people get hung up. Some people may think, "If my day starts later, then it doesn't matter." Wrong! It does matter. You may consider ending your workday a bit later to accommodate your late start. To us, this is about the freedom and flexibility we have as entrepreneurs.

Time is a funny thing. It will eat you alive if you allow it. You must ask and answer the KEY question, "What's most important to me in my life?" Then you set those things, foundationally, into your calendar and build from there.

The second question Traci asked herself...

2. *What logical boundaries must I establish and place around my precious blocks of time?*

This second question is very straightforward—it urges you to think about this thing called **boundaries**. We will implore you to develop a mindset that enables you to draw some important lines in the sand.

When you first decide what's truly most important to you, and you layer those things into your calendar (foundationally), you must **hold true** to those primacies. Okay...only a few exceptions...use Traci's rule. Ask, "Is it dead, dying or on fire?" If it isn't, then build an imaginary border wall around the blocks of time demarcated in your calendar, and don't let anyone or anything enter into it illegitimately. This should happen with ALL blocks of time, not just professional time.

> *"...build an imaginary border wall around the blocks of time demarcated in your calendar, and don't let anyone or anything enter into it illegitimately."*

Establishing and honoring boundaries around your precious blocks of professional time doesn't mean you are a bad parent or spouse. Conversely, if you shut off your mobile device and completely honor your sacred family time, it doesn't mean you are shirking your professional commitments. Creating logical boundaries that you ask your spouse and children to honor is a logical approach to managing the chaos of being a solopreneur. Likewise, the discipline of being 100% present for your family when that time comes each day, allows you to know in your heart that you are being the best mom, dad, husband or wife possible.

Please be aware that this practice will feel great until someone sticks his or her nose into the mix—they butt up against a foundational boundary. This scenario can and will include spouse and children. When this occurs, you'll simply have to train those around you what you'll allow inside of your time blocks and what you will not. This adjustment will be difficult for you. Even Traci's little (not so little anymore) six-year-old had to learn that mom wasn't there for her every whim and desire. She had to learn how to prepare for her day also.

Look, this isn't something you get right overnight; it's a work in progress. It's something you commit to every day when you wake up.

Back in the day we titled all of this stuff, 'time management.' However, we now dislike using that moniker because it seems impossible to us to actually MANAGE time. This is largely because of the unsolicited white noise coming at our eyes and ears. In addition, there are innumerable platforms that people can utilize to **reach** us. We believe that trying to manage time is a waste of time. We'd rather like you to lay the foundation for your **purposeful** use of time—realizing that it's a **living, breathing thing**. Time moves how we move, and it gives us what we give it.

"Time moves how we move, and it gives us what we give it."

As you begin to establish winning sales attitudes about **time**, we'll petition you to consider that the mindsets you choose to embrace in this area will probably be the deciding factor in whether you experience success or crash and burn failure. There are time choices we make in the moment. We choose what is important to us every second of every day— literally hundreds of times each day. What we'd like you to do is to take a **purposeful look** at your life, deciding what's truly important, while also identifying what's pilfering your time. This mindset will allow you to create **structure** to each of your days. It will assist you in putting a plan in place so that you know where you're going each week and you have the confidence that you are not short-changing anything or anyone, especially your loved ones.

So, a few closing questions to help you establish your mindset on time **primacy** and your **foundations** of time;

- How are you **using** your time currently?

- What does this **say** about you?
- Have you decided what's **truly important** to you?
- What **boundaries** will you need to establish?

Let's get this one right!

CHAPTER 29

Your Valuable Sands of Time

Our personal hourglass

JOE BUZZELLO

*"What's valuable to me has become clearer as I've gotten older. To me, it's about the **value** of your time and the value of the people you spend it with."*

—BRAD PITT

It's not uncommon in our world to applaud workaholics. We even hold them up as heroes.

You've seen this type of highly charged entrepreneur or independent salesperson. They race around, cantankerously announcing that they are exhausted, so "busy," "swamped," or "slammed." They'll tell you there isn't enough time to get everything done.

They think they're successful.

You think they're successful.

And they seem prosperous to the world. But, if you think about it, that really doesn't make much sense. You can only **TRULY** be successful if you can actually reap the benefits of your hard work.

Look, I'm probably the last person that should point fingers. I ran over seventy hours a week for close to two decades, never taking a true vacation. (A beeper or mobile device was always strapped to my side.) When I began to take stock of my life, I realized that I had not taken a vacation longer than seven days since I'd begun my commission-selling career in 1979. I'm not sure I was completely present to my wife and daughter during my go-go years. I still struggle with that now, even in semi-retirement.

As I have slowed a bit and crossed the line, joined the 55+ Club, I've started to look at things a little bit differently. **I value my time** more and place emphasis on the things that are really important to me. I'm not suggesting you lessen your commitment to your career or organization, I'm simply suggesting that it may be possible for you to strike more balance in your work and personal life. This, in turn, will even improve your work performance. **Instead of working harder, I recommend you learn to work smarter.**

I start my weekdays early, enjoying how quiet everything is. I'm able to focus on the tasks that need to get done. My routine is usually to work on a few creative things such as writing or editing content. I'll reply to the emails that have built up in my inbox. I make a game out of getting task-oriented things off my 'to-do' list before 8:00 am. This gives me more time later in the day for high ROI projects, calls that come in, or any unexpected issues. Because I stay highly productive during the week, I'm able keep my weekends mostly free.

Here are some thoughts on the VALUE of your time:

More Clarity/Better Judgment

The stark reality is that when you begin your sales career, new venture, or business, you're going to have to pump harder than you ever dreamed of. There aren't enough hours in the day. I can literally work around the clock and never whittle down my 'to-do' list! The more you do, or sell, the more decisions you have to make. My experience tells me that when I slow it down on the weekend, shut off my brain for a few hours and do something fun, I'm able to develop more clarity about business issues. I find that when I take the time to re-boot, I am able to make better decisions and find solutions on Monday morning.

Sunday Night LIVE

It SUCKS to be running around on Monday morning **without a clear agenda** of priorities for the week. If my calendar isn't airtight, I feel rattled and disorganized. I hated that feeling, so I started creating some focused planning time on Friday afternoon to look ahead to the next week and get my calendar wired. My big calendar checkpoint transpires on Sunday night. I'll spend 15 – 20 minutes Sunday evening, looking at my calendar, making sure I know where I'm going and what I'm going to focus on. I fine-tune. I make sure that I know what my **top priorities** are for the week. I make sure those items are INKED in my calendar. At first, I thought I was the only nut-job staring at my calendar on a Sunday night until I started checking around. What I found was that most of the elite producers were doing the very same thing.

Round Yourself Out

Most hard-charging salespeople and entrepreneurs understand that passion is a vital element to becoming successful. It's also important to follow your passions outside of work. Use your weekend to **explore your creative side**. The activity doesn't really matter. What's important is to take a break. These non-work-related pursuits will make you happier and a better-rounded person. This is another way to re-boot. You'll start your week with fresh batteries.

Maybe You Should Unplug?

I'm not great at meditating, but I'm learning different ways to clear my very busy head. But, it's hard to clear your head or relax if you are **tethered** to your personal electronic devices 24/7. Technology has made it difficult for us to unplug. One small step you can take is to keep your devices out of your hands and in a drawer on the weekends, at least for longer blocks of time.

A few years back I spent time with the best selling author, Jack Canfield. During a break, he told me that during a "FREE DAY" (for him that's a day he does ZERO work) he doesn't have any electronic devices near him. He's truly unplugged! After one day of observing me, sizing me up, Jack told me that he didn't think I could set down my phone and take a real free day. I'm still trying to prove him wrong...getting closer by the day. LOL!

If you think about it, most of us aren't saving lives. A patient isn't going to die if we miss a call or email. Everything will still be there when you get back to work. We live in a competitive world. Taking a break, some unaffected **FREE TIME** on the weekend will allow you to take a hard look at where you are and determine where you want to go next.

Functional Family

If you gain wealth, recognition, stature and power and then you lose your family, what have you really gained? You work hard because you want to give yourself and your family the best of everything. Sometimes the biggest sacrifice you'll have to make as an entrepreneur is spending limited time with your loved ones. Use the weekends to spend time with them. Take time out to get together with friends and socialize. Success means nothing if you're not able to share it with people that you love.

The Hourglass

Even though I'm suggesting that you take time off from work during the weekend, it is also critical not to waste your leisure time on mindless activities or doing chores. So, what I'm saying here is, try to work smarter, value and use your time better. Avoid **time vampires.** Quit checking your emails and unplug. Use your downtime to rejuvenate rather than exhaust yourself. Running a successful business is great, but taking care of your health and your family while doing things you love is also important.

I have a small **hourglass** on my bookcase in my home office. Once in a while I'll turn it upside down. I simply watch it as the sand drops through the small hole, at first slowly and then, at the end, the sand seems to drop faster. Then, the hourglass is still. There is no more sand, no more time.

The small hourglass is my reminder that time well spent with loved ones, doing the things that put a smile on our face, not just the pursuit of money or recognition, is by far, the most valuable commodity we have. You don't hear a person on their deathbed say, "I wish I could go into my office just one more Saturday and clean up some files." What they wish they could do is have one more week...heck, maybe just one more day, with the people they love, doing the things with them that were fulfilling.

If you are still not convinced that time well spent is more valuable than money, please read this poem, written by **Rinku Tiwari:**

*To realize the value of a **year**,*
Ask a student who failed in the exam.
*To realize the value of a **month**,*
Ask a mother how she spends the first month with her child.
*To realize the value of a **week**,*
Ask a patient how he recovers from his illness.
*To realize the value of an **hour**,*
Ask a student who missed the class.
*To realize the value of a **minute**,*
Ask a person who missed the train.
*To realize the value of a **second**,*
Ask a person who saved you from an accident.
*To realize the value of a **millisecond**,*
Ask a person who has won the medal in the competition.

ACKNOWLEDGEMENTS

(Lots of "thank you" stuff to some awesome people)

*"Many ideas grow better when **transplanted** into another mind than the one where they sprang up."*

—OLIVER WENDELL HOLMES

I love the quote above.
It fits so well with what happened to *cause* this book.

The ideas for chapters that could explain (and teach) the many attitudes we dove into came from **the minds of OTHERS**. Then...they were **transplanted** into my mind, and then that contributor and I would move the content back and forth until the collaboration was done. This marks the first time I've placed my author name next to others...and I'm feeling like it worked out pretty well! So let's get onto the business of thanking my talented co-authors. (In alphabetical order)

Talk about attitude! **Katie Anderson** has been one of the most grateful and positive people that I've ever had the opportunity to work with. She was a sponge during this process—a glutton for mentorship. She is

223

the kind of person that will tackle big, new challenges without any fear... or maybe she hides it well. LOL! Thanks for always putting a smile on my face with all of your kind and funny notes, Katie. You are a real talent!

Have you ever met somebody that isn't afraid to voice or show their emotions regardless of what the heck they are feeling? **Traci Batten** is one of those people. Traci is 100% authentic—very much in touch with what she's feeling. She also has a hunger for helping people, and that characteristic, combined with her emotional awareness, makes it easy for her to place words on paper. If I were a betting man, I'd wager that she will write a 'solo' book sooner than later. Thanks for all the laughs, and for always being REAL, Traci.

I first met **Renee Corso** when she was two days old and I was two years old. We are first cousins, but she's more like the little sister that I never had the chance to tease. Renee is intense. It's hard for me to name somebody that cares more about being a great sales leader than Renee. In addition, she really gets people, and I think this makes her a great coach and mentor. Thanks for being part of this book...and part of my life, Renee. You and Willie are so special to us.

Then there is **Leon Davidson**. Leon is a Cubs fan, so he's been in constant therapy for the last four decades. LOL! All kidding aside, he is a marvelous spirit, extremely jovial, but he doesn't seem to be the guy who feels the needs to be the center of attention. He's an extremely keen listener—almost kind of quiet—maybe introspective. Then...when you least expect it, he'll come off the wall with a great idea, concept or question. He has a ton of wisdom and it is so much fun to be able to work with him. Thanks for being YOU, Leon...and GO DODGERS!

Sometimes you meet a person, and you know they have a great deal of talent...but then you realize that they aren't 100% aware of how much potential they have. **Emily Evans** is one of those—a real diamond in the rough—just beginning to realize what she is capable of. Emily has a great deal of resolve to move her career forward and take others with her. What a pleasure it is to work with her. So a big "thank you" for all of your energy and talent, Emily.

As long as we are on the subject of resolve, I'll toss **Chuck Farmer** into the conversation. I think Chuck wakes up in the morning 100% pumped—as soon as his eyes open—he's ready to kill it. I'm not sure how old Chuck is. He can be anywhere from thirty-five years old to about seventy—I'm just not sure. LOL! He certainly has more energy than most thirty-five year olds. The word that I use most often to describe Chuck is, GRIT. He's 100% committed to getting his job done. He is a genuine character, but more importantly, he is a BIG talent—one of the most inspirational people I've met in over two decades. Thanks for being part of this book, Chuck. Give Ruthie a hug for me. Lots more to come!

I have known **Dennis Hartin** for many years now. A nicer, more helpful person you will never meet. He is one of those guys that will go out of his way to make your world a better place. He is one of the most gifted servant leaders I've ever observed. He is also a great industry leader and thinker. Dennis (like me) was not afraid to reinvent himself right in the middle of his career. There are more BIG wins ahead for Dennis…I can't wait to be a small part of them. Thanks for your and Brandy's friendship over the years, and for being part of this book, Dennis!

I got to know **Brandee Justus** as we began our CAP Equation Certified Instructor (CECI) program in early 2019. I immediately observed that Brandee had a huge heart for people—realizing that she cared greatly about others on her team—it was all about them experiencing success. Brandee is also one of those, 'Diamond in the Rough' people—a person that will have a lot of success writing, speaking and coaching. Thank you Brandee…you put a smile on my face each time we speak!

Christie Marzari and I met many, many years ago. We worked with the same organization and traveled in the same late-night circles of trust. These were those marathon evenings where unbelievable stories were shared, and new whacky memories were created on the spot, with the help of a few cocktails. She has been a professional sales trainer for over two decades. I guess you can say that she's dedicated her entire adult life to equipping salespeople to succeed. She is one of the most talented sales coaches I know, and I want to thank her for her hard work on this book and also for simply being a great friend over the years!

Scott Storjohann is also one of those people that I didn't have the pleasure of meeting prior to his involvement in our **CAP Equation** instructor group. Scott is a master salesperson. His contribution to this book became one of the meatiest and strongest chapter lessons that we featured. One of the BEST things that emanated for me from the writing of this book was getting to connect with people like Scott. Thanks so much for your work on this content, Scott! Lots more to come for you, also.

Last, but certainly not least; I'd like to thank **Dawn Tyack**. I want to thank Dawn for quite a few things. First, she and her husband, Andy, have been great and supportive friends—always rooting me on! I don't know if she is aware of this, but she was my very first (official) personal coaching client. This means a lot to me and I want to thank her for that vote of confidence. Aside from thanking her for being a big part of this book, I lastly want to thank her for being willing to always tell me exactly what's on her mind. She is a person that is not afraid to challenge me. We all need that. You rock, Dawn!

The **connection** I've formed with all of these great contributors will last a lifetime, and that's not something I will take for granted.

I also want to thank all of the many awesome **supporters** of the work that we do. Every time I receive a comment from you, I smile. The strong tribe that we've built over the last five years has been just plain wonderful. I'm so thankful for all the people that tell me that they receive value from what we put out there. When somebody says, "Hey that was a life changing idea," well...there just isn't anything better than hearing that!

We don't want to forget the 'behind the scenes' heroes of this book. I'm always so relieved to hand over our finished draft to **Jerry Dorris** and his great team at **AuthorSupport.com**. They do such an awesome job with the cover concept and all of the interior design elements and industry standard formatting.

Thanks so much Jerry and team!

Beth. (My wonderful wife)

This book may have happened without her, but it would have probably sucked a little, here and there.

LOL!

Beth assumed a key role in the editing and structure of this book. The rough editing and structural flow became a big job for her and I. The reason for this is that we (for the first time) invited those 'other' voices into the mix. So, I had to share a light hand in the ghost writing function, while still maintaining a **style** that didn't jump wildly around from chapter to chapter. Beth had to look at the (almost) completed chapters and then make sure that she was picking up on any subtle **inconsistencies** that I had overlooked. Her acute judgment of what our readers want to see, make this book much better than it would have been.

In addition to her structural editing work, she regularly talks me off the ledge when I begin to second-guess my work. There's no author out there who hasn't said, or thought, "This is crap and nobody will read it!" LOL! Beth's gentle reassurance is always just what I need, just at the time I need it. So that's my secret sauce...Beth.

I love her so much. I can't thank her enough.

Okay.

I certainly have some strong and caring people around me. I try not to take them for granted.

I'm quite blessed.

I hope I haven't missed thanking anybody. ☺

Thank you so much for reading this book!

Joe

About Our Co-authors

Katie Anderson has invested the last eighteen years of her career in high-level sales leadership roles, serving in positions with corporations and non-profit organizations in multiple industries. Katie is the Co-Founder and Managing Partner of **Anderson Atwood Consulting, Inc** (AAC). AAC is a private  brokerage in Denver, Colorado focused on client service, outside the box business solutions and strategic benefits collaboration. Katie is passionate about education, teaching and coaching. She has a Bachelors Degree in English with an emphasis in writing and a minor in Communications from California State University, Channel Islands. She also holds two California Teaching Credentials. Katie can be reached at (303) 638-5150 or via email katie@andersonatwood.com

Traci Batten is a nationally recognized expert in B2B sales/marketing, entrepreneurial growth and organizational leadership. She's enjoyed over fifteen years of success in the small business arena and served in executive level leadership positions for several Fortune 500˙ companies. She has  been recognized for her record-setting sales production and leadership skills at a local and national level. Since stepping away from her corporate career, she has dedicated her efforts to serving high-level sales and business professionals that wish to grow their enterprises. In 2019, Traci founded **Traci Batten, LLC** and she's currently an Intuitive Coach/ Mentor and keynote speaker. Traci is studying for her degree in Bioenergy work and she's also certified in the specialized healing work of Ho' Oponopono, having had the privilege of working with and learning from Joe Vitale. Traci can be reached at (314) 365-8149 or via email at: tracibatten1@gmail.com

Renee Corso has spent over three decades in B2B sales and leadership roles, becoming a recognized expert in both areas. She began her career in the apparel industry developing national account relationships with Guess Jeans, Tommy Hilfiger and Juicy Couture. In 2006, Renee made a major industry  shift, transitioning into the insurance industry. Over the following decade she built a strong sales team in the Los Angeles area, eventually accepting a promotion to run a regional business unit for her company. Renee continued her successful journey by establishing her team as #1 in both recruiting and overall production while also earning top awards nationally in virtually every category. Renee resides in Burbank, CA. Renee can be reached at (213) 247-1751 or via email at: rsdibona.corso@gmail.com

Leon Davidson is a decorated sales leader for a Fortune 500 company in the greater Sacramento area. He is also a B2B sales expert having earned his CAP Equation Certified Instructor designation. (**CECI**)  Leon has had the unique experience of achieving success as both an entrepreneur and an employee. This allows him to offer perspective when engaging with anyone connected to a business. He is committed to the art and science of coaching salespeople. Leon can be reached at: (916) 475-6838 or at: Leondavidson@comcast.net

Emily Evans is a B2B sales expert, a successful entrepreneur and an inspirational leader. She specializes in assisting small business owners with human capital, benefits, and solutions. Emily has earned many national sales and leadership awards and was also nominated as Small Business Woman

of the Year in 2016. She is quite involved in her local community (Gilbert, AZ) where she serves as the chair of the Small Business Council for the Gilbert Chamber of Commerce. Emily is dedicated to building a legacy of servant leadership by helping entrepreneurial professionals grow. She has earned her CAP Equation Certified Instructor designation. (CECI') Emily can be reached at: (480) 535-2865 or by email at: eevans@emilyevans.biz

Chuck Farmer began his leadership journey with Cracker Barrel in an entry-level position while attending college. He was soon offered a management position at their corporate offices. Chuck became a leader in several other departments, including corporate training, employee training, loss prevention and operations. A good friend kept telling Chuck how much he'd enjoy the freedom and rewards that a commission sales position provided. He decided the move was worth the risk. Seventeen years later, he's glad he took that leap. Chuck is a decorated organizational leader with Aflac in Tennessee. He is also called upon to deliver keynote presentations and workshops across the country. While he's enjoyed the freedom, monetary rewards and rapid advancement, his favorite aspect of the business (and his passion) is helping people succeed. Chuck can be reached at: (616) 417-0611 or by email: chuck.farmer007@gmail.com

Dennis Hartin is the President of **Hartin Dynamics**, which is the culmination of years of service to his clients. Dennis started his insurance career in 1994 and quickly moved up the ranks with a national carrier, serving at multiple levels as a sales producer, coach and leader. He ultimately managed a sales team of over six hundred representatives and over one hundred million dollars in existing assets. Dennis has served in multiple roles with the National Association of Health Underwriters; he is a Certified "Leadership in Life Institute" Instructor with NAIFA, a Health Rosetta Certified advisor and a founding CAP Equation Certified Instructor. (CECI') Dennis currently serves on the board of Autism Shifts, connecting employers and trained students. He also served for many years with the Boy Scouts of America and Children's Dream Racer. He has a unique passion for helping others, whether in his profession, community or circle of friends and family. Dennis can be reached at: (727) 359-2148 or by email at: dennis@hartindynamics.com

Brandee Justus has invested over twenty years in high-level sales, marketing, and leadership positions. She has learned that authenticity is the key to personal and professional accomplishment. Brandee believes that clearly communicated, high expectations empower individuals and teams to perform beyond their perceived potential. She has deep experience in high-end boutique management, proprietary education, non-profit health agencies and the insurance industry. Throughout her career, she has received numerous awards and recognition for sales and leadership. Brandee grew up in Michigan and currently lives in southern Indiana with her husband of nearly twenty-five years, and their two teenage boys. She is a huge "mom fan" of local high school sports, an avid reader and volunteers for CASA. Brandee can be reached at: (317) 385-9314 or brandeejustus@gmail.com

Christie Marzari has dedicated her professional life to training and mentoring professional salespeople. She has a deep level of expertise in; sales process training, curriculum development, coaching methods, selling techniques, sales analytics, business development strategies and the overall business planning process. Christie has served in executive level roles, spending the majority of her career with Aflac, a Fortune 500' company, earning many national awards. Christie earned her Bachelor of Science–Business Administration at Columbus State University in Columbus, GA. She's also earned many professional certifications including her Life Office Management Association, Inc., Fellow–Life Management Institute, Professional Customer Service, and Insurance Agency Administration and her NAHU–Certified Patient Protection and Affordable Care Act designation. Christie has also earned her CAP Equation Certified Instructor designation. (CECI') She can be reached at: (404) 444-4986 or by email at: cmmarzari@gmail.com

Scott Storjohann has spent his entire professional career in sales and organizational leadership. His journey has taken him from the health and fitness business to the insurance and financial product industry, building business units in the states of Oregon, Washington and Colorado. He has specialized in designing inbound as well as outbound sales campaigns and direct marketing processes. Scott has spent the last decade in key management positions with Aflac, a Fortune 200' insurance product leader, and he's built substantial B2B markets for the company. In 2019, Scott earned his CAP Equation Certified Instructor designation. (CECI') He's excited about leveraging this piece of knowledge so that he can offer even more value, benefit and solutions to local small business owners in Colorado. Scott resides in Westminster, Colorado with his wife Amanda. He can be reached at (541) 390-1429 and scott.s.aflac@gmail.com.

Dawn Tyack is an entrepreneur, leader and a perpetual student. For nearly two decades, she's experienced tremendous success in the insurance industry. Her sales team has been celebrated as the number one account development team in her state and Dawn has been the recipient of numerous national awards. In 2014, she earned a CLF designation from the American College and is also honored to have earned her CAP Equation Certified Instructor (CECI') designation in 2019. Dawn currently resides on the central coast of California and is the mother of four children and a chocolate lab named Stella. She is thrilled at the opportunity to connect, to be inspired and inspire others on their own journey to professional success. Dawn can be reached at: (805) 709-2270 or you can send her an email at: Dawntyack@gmail.com

About Joe Buzzello

Joe Buzzello has had an amazing career that has spanned over forty years. He's a nationally recognized expert in sales, entrepreneurial growth, sales/marketing processes and organizational leadership. Joe has built $100,000,000 + business units for Fortune 500° companies, served in executive level leadership positions and has been inducted into corporate Halls of Fame. Since stepping away from his corporate career, Joe has dedicated his professional efforts to writing, speaking and business coaching. He founded several companies and platforms such as, **The Buzzello Group, Inc., SELsource.com, Advance AZ, LLC** and is a venture partner in several other start-up companies. In 2015, Joe released his first book designed to assist sales people and trainers. The book and programs are entitled, *The CAP Equation©*, *A Foolproof Formula for Unlimited Success in Sales*. The book was an Amazon bestseller and is a must-have in sales organizations throughout the U.S. Joe has also written a novel, *Drawing Circles* and has released two more non-fiction books, *A Life in Sales* and his latest, *Winning Sales Attitudes*. Joe has recently co-founded the premier virtual growth community for entrepreneurs, **growth10**, which is now 'home' for his branded sales and leadership content. joe@growth10.com

For additional resources GO TO: www.growth10.com

If you enjoyed reading

Winning Sales Attitudes

...and you want to grab more great resources and interact with any of our great co-authors, then please go to:

www.growth10.com

We are a virtual entrepreneurial growth community unlike any other. You can learn game-changing practices in less than 10 minutes, access vetted resources, go deeper with master class course work, or join private groups to engage and also gain feedback and valuable input on the issues that are important to you as you build your business.

Join us at: www.growth10.com

Other books written by Joe Buzzello:

THE CAP EQUATION

A Foolproof Formula for
Unlimited Success in Sales

DRAWING CIRCLES

A Novel
(Based on actual events)
Greed, Crime and Shattered Dreams

A LIFE IN SALES

VOLUME 1:
The Stone Age: 1978–1982
Mentors, Saints & Sinners – Wisdom,
Truths & Lies and The Incredible Lessons Learned

*Available on Amazon
in paperback and Kindle formats*